SIZING UP THE SOVIET ARMY

JEFFREY RECORD

SIZING UP THE SOVIET ARMY

THE BROOKINGS INSTITUTION

Washington, D.C.

Library of Congress Cataloging in Publication Data:
Record, Jeffrey.
  Sizing up the Soviet Army.
  (Studies in defense policy)
  Includes bibliographical references.
    1. Russia (1923–   U.S.S.R.). Armiya.   2. Russia
—Military policy.   I. Title.   II. Series.
UA772.R39   355.3'0947   75-26941
ISBN 0-8157-7367-6

9 8 7 6 5 4 3 2 1

THE BROOKINGS INSTITUTION is an independent organization devoted to nonpartisan research, education, and publication in economics, government, foreign policy, and the social sciences generally. Its principal purposes are to aid in the development of sound public policies and to promote public understanding of issues of national importance.

The Institution was founded on December 8, 1927, to merge the activities of the Institute for Government Research, founded in 1916, the Institute of Economics, founded in 1922, and the Robert Brookings Graduate School of Economics and Government, founded in 1924.

The Board of Trustees is responsible for the general administration of the Institution, while the immediate direction of the policies, program, and staff is vested in the President, assisted by an advisory committee of the officers and staff. The by-laws of the Institution state: "It is the function of the Trustees to make possible the conduct of scientific research, and publication, under the most favorable conditions, and to safeguard the independence of the research staff in the pursuit of their studies and in the publication of the results of such studies. It is not a part of their function to determine, control, or influence the conduct of particular investigations or the conclusions reached."

The President bears final responsibility for the decision to publish a manuscript as a Brookings book. In reaching his judgment on the competence, accuracy, and objectivity of each study, the President is advised by the director of the appropriate research program and weighs the views of a panel of expert outside readers who report to him in confidence on the quality of the work. Publication of a work signifies that it is deemed a competent treatment worthy of public consideration but does not imply endorsement of conclusions or recommendations.

The Institution maintains its position of neutrality on issues of public policy in order to safeguard the intellectual freedom of the staff. Hence interpretations or conclusions in Brookings publications should be understood to be solely those of the authors and should not be attributed to the Institution, to its trustees, officers, or other staff members, or to the organizations that support its research.

FOREWORD

The past decade and a half has witnessed a major strengthening of Soviet general-purpose forces. Although changes in the Soviet naval forces have received the most attention in the West, the ground forces have undergone no less significant a transformation. Moreover, the army—and how to deal with it in the event of hostilities—remains the principal preoccupation of NATO war planners.

In this study, the twelfth in the Studies in Defense Policy series, Jeffrey Record analyzes in some detail the character, capabilities, and strategy of the Soviet Army. He argues that a doctrinal fixation on short, intense war dominated by high-speed armored thrusts has resulted in a massive Soviet army with an immense initial punch; but that its lack of offensive staying power, strategic mobility, and technological prowess could eventually prove to be its undoing. He concludes, however, that such a military posture is well suited for central Europe, where the Soviet army confronts smaller, differently structured, and geographically restricted NATO forces.

Jeffrey Record is a research associate and former Rockefeller Younger Scholar on the defense analysis staff of the Brookings Foreign Policy Studies program, which is directed by Henry Owen. He is the author of *U.S. Nuclear Weapons in Europe: Issues and Alternatives* (1974), and coauthor of *U.S. Force Structure in NATO: An Alternative* (1974).

The Brookings Institution thanks Lieutenant Colonel William R. Ball, Colonel Paul Brown, Herbert S. Dinerstein, Dennis M. Gormley, Robert W. Komer, General Matthew B. Ridgway, Lewis D. Sargentich, and Thomas W. Wolfe for their helpful comments on this study. The author is also grateful for the suggestions of his Brookings colleagues Martin Binkin, Barry M. Blechman, Henry Owen, Alton M. Quanbeck, Archie L. Wood, and Joseph A. Yager; to Mendelle T. Berenson, who edited the manuscript; to Louisa Thoron, who checked the data and references; and to Christine Lipsey, who typed it.

The Institution acknowledges the assistance of the Ford Foundation, whose grant helps to support its defense and foreign policy studies. The views expressed here are the author's and should not be ascribed to those who commented on the study, to the Ford Foundation, or to the trustees, officers, or other staff members of the Brookings Institution.

KERMIT GORDON
President

August 1975
Washington, D.C.

CONTENTS

Text Tables

Text Figure

Appendix Table

CHAPTER ONE

INTRODUCTION

The size and character of the Soviet Army have been of grave concern to the United States and its European allies since the close of the Second World War. Indeed, the need to balance the Soviet Union's military power in Europe, particularly its large ground forces in Eastern Europe and in Russia's western military districts, remains the fundamental raison d'être of the North Atlantic Treaty Organization.

This study assesses the structure of the Soviet Army and the doctrine governing its use. Strengths and weaknesses are identified, as are certain recent trends within the army that many observers find disturbing in an era often cited as one of relaxing confrontation between East and West. Because of their crucial significance to Western military planners, those aspects of structure and doctrine that indicate the type of war that the Soviet Union is best prepared to wage receive particular attention.

The following chapter traces briefly the changing role of the army within the Soviet military establishment since 1945. Like other armies, the Soviet Army must compete with its sister services—the Strategic Rocket Forces, the Air Force, the Navy, and the Air Defense Command—for resources and prestige. Chapter 3 assesses the present structure and capabilities of Soviet ground forces and their implications for Soviet performance in a conflict. Admittedly, military capabilities do not necessarily reflect ultimate peacetime political intentions; however, they do offer a rough guide to objectives in the event of hostilities and to the manner in which they are likely to be pursued. Those objectives and the means of attaining them become even more apparent upon review of Soviet doctrine regulating the employment of its ground forces, which is the subject of chapter 4. The final chapter presents some conclusions as to the salient characteristics of the Soviet Army and their implications for the force posture of the United States. An appendix contains a brief sketch of the Soviet tactical-aviation posture and its relationship to land warfare.

CHAPTER TWO

THE ROLE OF THE SOVIET ARMY

The status of ground forces within the Soviet military establishment since the Second World War has reflected the evolving perceptions of the army's role in a future conflict. Those perceptions in turn have been shaped by two basic factors: (1) the restraining hand of historical traditions, many of which were "vindicated" in Russia's last and most profound military experience, the Great Patriotic War of 1941–45; and (2) the disrupting influence of technological advancement, particularly the revolution in destructive power wrought by the advent of nuclear weapons. The Soviet Army, like others, has discovered that history and technology are often at odds, and it is safe to say that the army's present character is largely the product of a series of compromises between the two influences.

The Postwar Stalinist Era: 1945–53

Russia's traditional focus on land warfare and its principal manifestation, the dominant role of the army within the Soviet military, emerged virtually unscathed from the Second World War. As a huge but technologically backward continental power historically independent of maritime communications in waging war, Russia had always sought security in a massive army designed to overwhelm smaller but usually more sophisticated opponents. Such naval and, later, air forces as Russia maintained appeared to be military "afterthoughts"; denied independent missions, both were designed principally to support land operations, and were utilized in that way. The Great Patriotic War seemed to corroborate the Soviet emphasis on a large army at the expense of other forms of military power. Victory over Nazi Germany, itself a continental giant whose renowned Luftwaffe also was configured mainly for close air support, was clearly won on the ground. Indeed, following the initial stages of the invasion of the USSR in the summer of 1941, air and naval power never played a decisive role on the Eastern Front.

An unshaken Soviet focus in the immediate postwar era on massive ground forces was coupled with a conviction that any new conflict involving the Soviet Union would, like the war just past, be protracted. This conviction was epitomized in the "Five Principles of Victory" first identified by Stalin in 1942 as the timeless foundation of Soviet military power: (1) security of rear areas through political stability, (2) good morale, (3) sufficient numbers of divisions and quality, (4) sufficient mass of equipment, and (5) high ability and skill of the officers.[1] These principles remained the bible of Soviet military thought until the dictator's death in 1953, and suffocated the increasingly warranted revision of doctrine in the face of growing U.S. nuclear capabilities and the advent of the USSR's own nuclear forces.

Although Stalin publicly derided Western claims that atomic weapons had rendered traditional modes of warfare—if not war itself—obsolete, he undertook a crash program to achieve nuclear status for the USSR, resulting in detonation of the Soviet Union's first atomic bomb in 1949.[2] Nevertheless, the Soviet Army's dominance within the military remained unchallenged. Tradition aside, large ground forces were required to consolidate the new Soviet empire in Eastern Europe. More important, until the Soviets developed a credible strategic retaliatory capability, to deter the United States "Stalin's main recourse in the military field lay in making the threat of Soviet land power against Europe the counterpoise to U.S. nuclear power."[3] And the credibility of that threat lay in the maintenance of vast ground forces, the bulk of which seemingly was poised for the rapid conquest of West Europe.

The Khrushchev Era: 1953–64

The eleven years between Stalin's death and the fall of Khrushchev were a transitional period that witnessed profound changes both in mili-

---

1. Edgar O'Ballance, *The Red Army: A Short History* (Praeger, 1964), p. 192.
2. In 1946 Stalin stated, "I do not believe the atomic bomb to be a serious force as certain politicians are inclined to regard it. Atomic bombs are intended to intimidate the weak-nerved, but they cannot decide the outcome of war, since atomic bombs are by no means sufficient for this purpose." Quoted in Malcolm Mackintosh, *Juggernaut: A History of the Soviet Armed Forces* (Macmillan, 1967), p. 278.
3. Thomas W. Wolfe, *Soviet Power and Europe, 1945–1970* (Johns Hopkins Press, 1970), p. 34.

tary doctrine and in the structure of the armed forces. Doctrinally, the belief that ground forces were the crucial element in war gradually gave way to a new dogma that heralded the primacy of nuclear weapons in a potential conflict with the West and relegated ground forces to a supporting but not decisive role. Moreover, deterrence supplanted defense as the proclaimed bedrock of Russian security. Structurally, the Khrushchev era was characterized by the ascendance of the Strategic Rocket Forces as the paramount and most prestigious arm of the Soviet military and by progressive cuts in the size of the armed forces totaling about 50 percent. Reductions in the Soviet Army, however, were in part offset by an impressive modernization of its arms and equipment, including the introduction of tactical nuclear weapons within selected combat units.

These changes, which did not come easily, were driven by Khrushchev's firm belief that nuclear weapons had revolutionized warfare. Khrushchev's proposals to reduce ground forces and reorient the Soviet military posture toward deterrence based on the USSR's growing strategic nuclear arsenal encountered stiff opposition every step of the way. Tradition-bound elements within the Soviet military rejected Khrushchev's contention that in the nuclear era a successful defense rested not upon the number of soldiers under arms but upon the total firepower and the means of delivery. Until the end of 1957 at least, the "traditionalists" retained their faith in the decisiveness of a massive army and clung to a vision of future war as a protracted conflict. Opposing the "traditionalists" were the "modernists" —strongly supported by Khrushchev—who, as depicted in the text table on page 5, believed that nuclear ordnance and ballistic missiles had so changed warfare as to make large ground forces not merely unnecessary but a liability.

"Modernist" demands for reductions in Soviet ground forces arose from a presumption that any conflict with the USSR's principal adversary would be a short, extremely violent struggle whose ultimate outcome would be determined by initial nuclear exchanges. Brevity of combat would preclude the use of the full weight of ground forces by either side; indeed, large land formations would provide tempting and easy targets for nuclear strikes. The "traditionalists" argued that a large army was necessary precisely in order to absorb the huge losses anticipated in a nuclear environment.

By the early 1960s the "modernist" view clearly prevailed, a development facilitated by major changes in the Soviet High Command under the constant prodding of Khrushchev. The Soviet military widely agreed that nuclear weapons were crucial and that the initial stages of a conflict would decide its outcome. The implications for the army were explicit: relegation within the Soviet military to the secondary functions of exploiting the huge holes blasted in the enemy's defense by the Strategic Rocket Forces, mopping up surviving pockets of resistance, and occupying territory thus obtained—a relegation that entailed loss of status and of bureaucratic clout.

Issue	*"Traditionalists"*	*"Modernists"*
Strategic emphasis	defense	deterrence
Character of conflict		
Decisive element	quantity of ground forces	firepower/delivery systems
Role of nuclear weapons	not decisive	decisive
Warning time	adequate	none (surprise attack)
Importance of initial period	not decisive	decisive
Duration	protracted	short
Ground forces		
Role	primary	secondary
Size	massive	reduced

The influence of the "modernist" school was evident in the major cuts imposed upon the Soviet armed forces from 1955 through 1961. As shown in table 2-1, three separate programs of troop reduction initiated by

Table 2-1. Actual and Planned Troop Reductions within the Soviet Armed Forces, 1955–64

Thousands of men

Period	Prereduction strength	Size of cut		Postreduction strength	
		Actual	Planned	Actual	Planned
1955–57	5,763	1,840	1,840	3,923	3,923
1958–59	3,923	300	300	3,623	3,623
1960–61	3,623	600	1,200	3,023	2,423
1963– ?[a]	3,023	0	600	3,023	2,423
Total reduction	...	2,740	3,940	3,023	...

Sources: Michael Garder, *A History of the Soviet Army* (Praeger, 1966), p. 141; Thomas W. Wolfe, *Soviet Power and Europe, 1945–1970* (Johns Hopkins Press, 1970), pp. 164–66; and Edgar O'Ballance, *The Red Army: A Short History* (Praeger, 1964), p. 199.

a. The 1963 reduction program, which was never realized, was apparently designed to complete the only partially achieved program of 1960–61.

Khrushchev cut the armed forces by over 2,740,000 personnel during this period. A fourth program apparently was planned but never realized. Of significance is that these major cuts were not reflected in the Soviet garrison in Eastern Europe, which is believed to have been reduced by only 89,000 men from 1955 to 1963.[4] The influence of the "modernist" school also was evident in a significant reduction in artillery pieces and logistics stores, changes made presumably to enhance the mobility and invulnerability of ground units in nuclear war.[5]

The contraction of the army, however, was coupled with major qualitative improvements designed to ensure the effective participation of Soviet ground forces in nuclear combat. Tactical nuclear surface-to-surface missiles were introduced into the army and measures were undertaken to protect ground troops from the thermal and radiological effects of nuclear explosives. Battlefield tactics were adjusted to emphasize dispersal rather than concentration. Moreover, the mobility and conventional firepower of Soviet ground formations were substantially enhanced by mechanization of infantry divisions and by the introduction of superior tanks and other armored fighting vehicles.

Trends under Brezhnev

The past decade of Soviet military policy has been characterized by three major developments: (1) the attainment of a secure strategic nuclear retaliatory capability against the United States; (2) an attempt "to break out of the bounds of the continental Eurasian geostrategic shell without relying directly on intercontinental missiles";[6] and (3) a dramatic resurgence of traditional emphasis on ground forces and conventional capabilities.

Resurrection of the relative importance of ground forces was highlighted by a net addition of some twenty divisions to the army and by the restoration in 1967 of a separate command for Soviet ground forces. The command had been abolished by Khrushchev in 1964 and ground forces subordinated directly to the Ministry of Defense. The underlying causes of

4. Wolfe, *Soviet Power and Europe,* p. 166.
5. Dennis M. Gormley, "NATO's Tactical Nuclear Option: Past, Present and Future," *Military Review,* vol. 53 (September 1973), p. 10.
6. Andro Gabelic, "New Accent in Strategy," *Military Review,* vol. 48 (August 1968), p. 84.

these new developments were growing recognition of the unusability of strategic nuclear arms and at least tentative acceptance of the proposition that even a nuclear war in Europe need not necessarily provoke a strategic exchange, and that, if it did not, the army, as the principal repository of Soviet tactical nuclear capabilities, would play a decisive role.

The new Kremlin leadership, in addition, was

by no means pleased to have inherited a situation in which for two decades the United States not only enjoyed marked strategic superiority over the Soviet Union but also went virtually unchallenged in its capacity to intervene locally in contested trouble spots around the globe.[7]

The desire to extend the reach and enhance the flexibility of Soviet military power on a global basis has resulted in a substantial upgrading of the role of Soviet general-purpose forces. The Soviet Navy has been transformed from a mere appendage of land power into an instrument designed partially to support Soviet transoceanic political interests. Stress on reach and flexibility is no less apparent in ground forces and is manifest in the growing attention to airborne warfare and to strategic airlift capabilities. The results of these and other changes are the subject of the next chapter.

7. Wolfe, *Soviet Power and Europe*, p. 127.

CHAPTER THREE

THE SOVIET ARMY TODAY: PROFILE AND TRENDS

The Soviet Army is the most powerful army in the world. The product of both modern technology and peculiar historical experiences, it is undergoing changes that have serious implications for the military posture of potential adversaries. The purpose of this chapter is to present a profile of the Soviet Army and to identify significant trends within it. Also discussed are issues of continuing importance to Western military observers, such as Soviet mobilization capacity and ratios of combat to support troops. A review of the strategy and doctrine now governing the use of Soviet ground forces is provided in chapter 5.

Besides the army, Soviet ground forces include 180,000 border troops of the KGB (Committee of State Security), 130,000 MVD (Ministry of State Security) security troops, and 17,000 naval infantry distributed among the USSR's four fleets. Conceivably, these forces could be employed, as they were in some cases during World War II, to support Soviet Army operations; however, they cannot credibly be included in the Soviet land order of battle and are thus not covered in this study. The small and scattered naval infantry do not possess the capacity for amphibious assault beyond the range of Soviet land-based aviation. Although KGB and MVD forces are equipped with armored fighting vehicles, they are essentially paramilitary formations whose principal functions are to police Soviet borders, and in the event of war, to secure rear areas and to uphold the authority of the Soviet state within both the military and civilian populations. During the Second World War, for example, NKVD border troops (the predecessor of KGB border forces) "were not normally used in the forefront of battle, but formed the garrison of vital centres or were held back to round up stragglers or threaten Red Army units which were in danger of breaking."[1]

1. Albert Seaton, *The Russo-German War 1941–1945* (Praeger, 1971), p. 82.

Size

A striking aspect of the Soviet Army is its sheer size. Containing 1.8 million men organized around 56 full-strength divisions and 111 divisions of lesser readiness, the Red Army is second in size only to the Chinese People's Liberation Army, which now contains 2.5 million men and 197 divisions.[2] Moreover, although army manpower has remained fairly constant since 1967, the number of divisions has steadily expanded from 136 to 167, or almost 23 percent. This expansion is attributable for the most part to the buildup in recent years of Soviet Army forces opposite the Chinese border, a buildup that was achieved principally through the creation of new divisions rather than the redeployment of existing divisions.

The magnitude of the Soviet Army is rooted in the traditional Russian emphasis on quantitative preponderance, discussed in chapter 5. It is also a function of "the absence of a doctrinal or conceptual limit on the size and composition [of Soviet arms, which] derives from the fact that the Soviet forces are not designed primarily for deterrence but for war fighting purposes."[3] In fact, the dimensions of the Soviet Army do not appear excessive, given the size of the ground forces of the nation's principal potential adversaries. For example, the active manpower of NATO ground forces now deployed in Europe totals approximately 2 million personnel organized around no fewer than sixty division equivalents, most of which are 30 to 40 percent larger than Soviet divisions. These figures do not include U.S. Army formations in the United States, even those that are earmarked for European contingencies.

Inclusion of the Chinese Army increases the total ground-force threat to the Soviet Union to some 4.5 million personnel and approximately 257 divisions. Thus, from a strictly quantitative standpoint, it is easy to understand why Soviet military planners might view a war on two fronts as preeminently the "worst case." Aside from the great distance separating central Europe and the Far East, Soviet forces strategically would be collectively outnumbered by their adversaries by ratios of 2.5 to 1 in man-

2. Unless otherwise specified, data on the Soviet armed forces appearing in this study were obtained from *The Military Balance,* an annual publication of the International Institute for Strategic Studies, in London. The Institute will be referred to as IISS.

3. Leon Gouré, Foy D. Kohler, and Mose L. Harvey, *The Role of Nuclear Forces in Current Soviet Strategy* (University of Miami, Center for Advanced International Studies, 1974), p. 71.

power and 1.5 to 1 in divisions. Even complete mobilization of the USSR's estimated 9 million trained army reserves would little affect the unfavorable manpower balance, for it could be offset by a call-up of the Chinese Army's 5 million trained reserves and by mobilization of the 3,250,000 reserves available to European members of NATO alone.[4]

Recruitment and Training

Manpower for the Soviet Army is provided by a system of universal military service.[5] Under the provisions of the current law, which went into effect in 1968, men are conscripted at age eighteen for a minimum of two years' active duty. The previous system drafted nineteen-year-olds for a period of three years. The term of service was reduced apparently in an effort to allow more manpower to be trained for the civilian economy, and is believed to have been vigorously opposed by the Soviet military,[6] which not unjustifiably feared an erosion of training standards and a consequent lowered readiness. Perhaps as a form of compensation, pre-induction training has been substantially upgraded.

Unlike Western nations, the Soviet Union has assigned much of the responsibility for military training to organizations outside the armed services. Youths from sixteen to eighteen receive compulsory training at facilities located at their schools, factories, and farms. These programs are administered mainly by the All-Union Voluntary Society for Assistance to the Army, Air Force, and Navy (known as DOSAAF), an institution of 40 million people that operates through some 300,000 primary organizations. Instructors are reserve military officers, and the curriculum includes drill, familiarization with small arms, knowledge of military regulations, and cartography. The standard DOSAAF program of 140 classroom hours supplemented by a week or two of field exercises each summer does facilitate post-induction training, although it is a poor substitute for an

4. Trevor N. Dupuy, John A. C. Andrews, and Grace P. Hayes, *The Almanac of World Military Power* (3rd ed., T. N. Dupuy Associates, 1974), pp. 161, 282.

5. This section relies heavily upon information contained in Herbert Goldhammer, *Soviet Military Management at the Troop Level*, A Report Prepared for United States Air Force Project Rand, R-1513-PR (RAND Corporation, 1974).

6. James A. Barry, Jr., "Military Training of Soviet Youth," *Military Review*, vol. 53 (February 1973), p. 92.

additional year's service in the regular military. According to one observer, it is clear that the DOSAAF is not supplying a mass infusion of highly trained soldiers. The impact of their programs is probably better described as taking some of the basic and elementary technical training burden off the shoulders of an already overworked military training establishment.[7]

Once inducted into the army, conscripts are subjected to a rigorous training program that encompasses both military skills and politico-ideological indoctrination. However, the *degree* to which the post-induction program enhances readiness and combat effectiveness is the subject of debate. One student of the Soviet training process has concluded that the

heavy investment in political indoctrination has negative effects on attainable skill levels both by detracting from the time available for skill training and by establishing political priorities that reduce the skill return on the time that is devoted to technical training.[8]

Another weakness often cited by Western military analysts is the army's failure to use in training the actual equipment that it plans to use in combat, a policy that breeds unfamiliarity on the part of crews with the idiosyncrasies of the equipment they would be assigned in wartime.[9] The policy also reduces the capacity to maintain that equipment in a state of combat readiness. Finally, the absence since 1945 of a war directly involving the Soviet Union, while perhaps a tribute to Soviet diplomacy, has nevertheless deprived the military of all but vicarious access to the "laboratory" of combat that is so crucial for testing new weapons and tactics.

Structure

The Soviet Army contains three types of divisions: motorized rifle, armored, and airborne.

The USSR currently maintains 110 motorized rifle divisions (MRDs). These formations are the Soviet counterpart of U.S. mechanized infantry divisions, and at full strength muster 12,000 personnel. As table 3-1 shows, MRDs account for most of the divisions that have been added to the Soviet Army since 1967. The 50 armored divisions (ADs), although

7. Ibid., p. 96.
8. Goldhammer, *Soviet Military Management*, pp. 70–71.
9. Michael S. Davison, "The Military Balance in Central Army Group," *Strategic Review,* vol. 2 (Fall 1974), p. 16.

Table 3-1. Numbers of Soviet Army Divisions, by Type, 1965–74[a]

Year	Motorized rifle	Armored	Airborne	Total
1965	90	50	7	147
1966	90	43	7	140
1967	86	43	7	136
1968	88	45	7	140
1969	90	50	7	147
1970	100	50	7	157
1971	102	51	7	160
1972	106	51	7	164
1973	107	50	7	164
1974	110	50	7	167

Source: IISS, *The Military Balance, 1965–1966* through *1974–1975* (London: IISS, 1965 through 1974).
a. Includes divisions maintained at substantially less than full strength.

somewhat smaller (9,500 personnel at full strength), represent not only the largest tank force in the world but also the core of the army's shock power and offensive capabilities.

An inherently offensive orientation also distinguishes the army's seven airborne divisions (AbDs), each of which has 7,000 personnel and is kept in the highest state of readiness. Indeed, the maintenance of such sizable airborne forces by the USSR at a time when the military establishments of the United States and Western European nations are increasingly dubious of the future of the airborne mission[10] suggests a singular view on the part of the Russians that "the introduction of nuclear weapons into Soviet and Western armies" has *enhanced* the value of airborne forces because they represent "a means of consolidating the results of nuclear strikes . . . and of opening a 'new front' to aid in the exploitation of these strikes by conventional tank and mechanized units."[11]

Growth has characterized not only the number of divisions within the army but also the size of each division. Although the authorized tank strength for both types of divisions has actually declined, manpower assigned to MRDs and ADs has expanded since 1967 (see table 3-2). The explanation for increases in division manpower remains obscure. The fact

10. The 82nd Airborne Division is the only airborne formation left in the U.S. Army. The old 101st Airborne Division, now redesignated the 101st Air Assault Division, lost all vestiges of airborne capability in 1973. Great Britain, France, and Germany maintain even smaller airborne forces.

11. Graham H. Turbiville, "Soviet Airborne Troops," *Military Review,* vol. 53 (April 1973), p. 61.

Table 3-2. Manpower and Medium Tanks in Full-Strength Soviet Army Divisions, by Type, 1965–74

Year	Manpower (*thousands*)			Medium tanks[a]	
	Motorized rifle	Armored	Airborne	Motorized rifle	Armored
1965	11.0	9.0	7.0	210	375[b]
1966	11.0	9.0	7.0	210	375[b]
1967	10.5	9.0	7.0	190	350
1968	10.5	9.0	7.0	190	350
1969	10.5	8.5	7.0	180	319
1970	10.0	8.3	7.0	175	325
1971	10.5	8.4	7.0	175	325
1972	10.0	9.0	7.0	188	316
1973	10.8	9.0	7.0	188	316
1974	12.0	9.5	7.0	188	325

Sources: *Military Balance, 1965–1966* through *1974–1975*.
a. No medium tanks are assigned to airborne divisions.
b. Includes heavy tanks.

that until recently Soviet divisions were, in terms of men although not tanks or artillery tubes, little more than one-half the size of U.S. and Western European divisions possibly may have stimulated expansion, although a desire to mimic Western ground-force organization and structure has rarely been evident in Soviet Army force planning. Undoubtedly, the demand for mechanics and other maintenance-support personnel has increased as the army has acquired more sophisticated equipment. Moreover, the Russians may have recognized that their low ratio of infantry to armor could make their MRDs and ADs highly vulnerable when operating in close country, where rapid movement is difficult.

Even more curious is the failure to use the additional manpower to create new formations or to flesh out understrength divisions. Presumably, new divisions rather than larger old ones would be more visible and therefore more valuable bargaining chips in negotiations on the mutual reduction of forces in Europe, now taking place in Vienna. Similar political benefits also might have been derived had the additional manpower been used to enhance the readiness of the many Soviet divisions that remain understrength.

The unparalleled degree to which the USSR has organized its ground forces around the tank is reflected in the comparative ratios of tanks to men within divisions, particularly armored divisions, shown in table 3-3.

Table 3-3. Ratio of Medium Tanks to Men in Motorized Infantry and Armored Divisions of the Soviet Union, United States, West Germany, and Great Britain, 1974

Type of division and country	Tanks	Men	Ratio of tanks to men
Motorized infantry			
Soviet Union	188	12,000	1:64
United States[a]	216	16,300	1:75
West Germany	250	15,500	1:62
Great Britain[b]	200	12,500	1:63
Armored			
Soviet Union	325	9,500	1:29
United States	324	16,500	1:51
West Germany	300	14,500	1:48
Great Britain[b]	200	12,500	1:63

Source: Author's calculations based on data appearing in *Military Balance, 1974–1975*, p. 83.

a. The U.S. Army also maintains three unmechanized infantry divisions, two of which contain only one tank battalion of fifty-four tanks, giving them a tank–men ratio of 1:302.

b. British divisions are shown here as identical although their composition can vary.

The Soviet ratio suggests not only deliberate preparation for high-speed offensive operations but also a comparatively low capability to sustain such operations over an extended period of time. Indeed, the proportion of tanks to men is but one expression of a remarkably high overall ratio of combat to support troops within the Soviet Army. This phenomenon is discussed further below.

The magnitude of Soviet investment in mobility and shock power is further evident in the number and types of maneuver battalions within the Red Army. Maneuver battalions are the principal repository of an army's offensive and counterattack capability. Unlike the functions of other formations such as artillery, reconnaissance, engineer, and medical units, the purpose of maneuver battalions is to close with and destroy the enemy in combat. As table 3-4 reveals, upon complete mobilization the Soviet Army would contain five times the number of maneuver battalions that are now assigned to all U.S. Army divisions, separate brigades, and National Guard and reserve units. Although Soviet battalions are less than half the size of U.S. battalions, their structure and the operational doctrine governing their use have led at least one observer to conclude that "these small battalions are capable of projecting shock power comparable with that of the larger NATO battalion."[12] The reason is that

12. Steven L. Canby, *NATO Military Policy: Obtaining Conventional Comparability with the Warsaw Pact*, A Report Prepared for Defense Advanced Research Projects Agency, R-1088 (RAND Corporation, June 1973), pp. 13–14.

Table 3-4. U.S. and Soviet Army Force Structure, by Number and Type of Maneuver Battalions, All Active and Reserve Formations

| | U. S. Army[a] | | | | Soviet Army, 1974[b] | |
| | Fiscal year 1975 | | Fiscal year 1977 | | | |
Type of maneuver battalion	Number	Percent of total	Number	Percent of total	Number	Percent of total
Infantry	110	32	123	33	...	...
Mechanized infantry	90	27	97	26	784	46
Armored	92	27	102	27	850	51
Airborne	11	3	11	3	49	3
Other[c]	36	11	39	11	...	...
Total	339	100	372	100	1,683	100

Sources: Author's calculations based on information supplied by Defense Department sources and on data appearing in *Military Balance, 1974–1975*, p. 83.
a. Includes battalions in active divisions and separate brigades, and in National Guard, affiliated reserve, and nonaffiliated reserve units.
b. Upon full mobilization of all Soviet divisions.
c. Armored cavalry and air cavalry battalions.

the Soviets fight for impact, and their units in the attack below the regimental level deploy almost their entire infantry and tank strength with specialized antitank units functioning as reserves. NATO practice is to deploy two-thirds of each unit, leaving a third in reserve—a practice that snowballs into a front-line division having only 18 percent of its tank and infantry strength on line and 82 percent in reserves at various command levels; the comparable Soviet percentages are 30 on line and 70 in reserve. Consequently, in circumstances where the Soviets have the initiative and can employ their shock power tactics so that their battalions have hitting power comparable with NATO's, they are able to lever up their small divisions to an effectiveness level approaching their advantage in maneuver battalions.[13]

Moreover, 51 percent of Soviet maneuver battalions are tank battalions compared with only 27 percent for the United States.

Of perhaps even greater import is the fact that all Soviet infantry formations are mechanized, whereas 110, or 55 percent, of U.S. active and reserve infantry battalions (excluding airborne battalions) remain dependent mainly upon marching for their overland mobility.[14]

13. Ibid., p. 14.
14. By the close of fiscal 1977 the U.S. Army will contain five unmechanized infantry divisions—the 2nd, 25th, 9th, 7th, and 24th. The 82nd Airborne and 101st Air Assault divisions also may be classified as infantry divisions insofar as they lack sufficient ground transport for their maneuver battalions. A standard infantry division possesses few tracked vehicles; as for organic "soft-wheeled" mobility items such as trucks, the accepted rule of thumb is that only one brigade of three infantry

The significance of complete mechanization in the form of either tracked personnel carriers or wheeled vehicles becomes apparent upon perusal of the structure of German ground forces assembled for the Nazi invasion of Russia in June 1941. Although *Barbarossa* (the German code name for the invasion) remains the largest and one of the most spectacular examples of blitzkrieg warfare, contrary to popular impression it was undertaken by an army that not only was largely unmotorized but also contained comparatively few armored units. The German order of battle for *Barbarossa* was as follows: 111 unmotorized infantry divisions, 1 cavalry division, 14 motorized infantry (Panzer Grenadier) divisions, and 19 armored (Panzer) divisions, for a total of 145 divisions. Thus, only 33 divisions (14 motorized infantry and 19 armored), or 23 percent of the entire invasion force, were motorized. The remaining divisions, with the exception of a single cavalry division, were essentially "foot" formations of the World War I type, dependent on horse-drawn vehicles for movement of their supplies and equipment. The Third Reich's failure to put its infantry on wheels or tracked vehicles has been cited by many military analysts as a major cause of the disaster that subsequently befell German arms on the Eastern Front.[15]

As table 3-4 also shows, these and other asymmetries in force structure between the Soviet and U.S. armies will be little affected by the projected expansion of the U.S. Army from thirteen to sixteen divisions by the close of fiscal year 1977. Two of the three new divisions will be "straight-legged" infantry divisions (that is, infantry divisions dependent mainly upon marching for their mobility), although there are indications that at some point during the next decade they will be mechanized. Moreover, the addition of thirty-three active maneuver battalions will only slightly improve the present quantitative imbalance in those formations.

Nor is a sixteen-division U.S. Army—despite an unchanged aggregate manpower level—likely to lead to a dramatic increase in the compara-

---

battalions and its assigned equipment can be moved at one time. Moreover, only 30 percent of that lift capability could be provided by the battalions themselves; the remaining 70 percent would have to come from supply and transport elements in the division base.

These figures assume an 80 percent availability of all trucks within an infantry division; but even on this high assumption, only one brigade's worth of men and equipment could be transported. Food, fuel, and ammunition would have to be moved by other means.

15. See, for example, Larry H. Addington, *The Blitzkrieg Era and the German General Staff, 1865–1941* (Rutgers University Press, 1971).

tively low ratio of combat ("teeth") to support ("tail") troops traditional to U.S. ground forces. In sharp contrast is the Soviet Army's high ratio of combat to support, whose implications for NATO war planning remain a major issue in the West. The long-standing "teeth-to-tail" controversy is complicated by the myriad definitions of combat and support troops. Yet, by almost any criterion, the Soviet Army musters one of the highest ratios in the world. For example, if men in divisions are counted as combat troops and those outside divisions as support, then the Soviet Army possesses a combat-to-support ratio of 71 to 29[16] compared to a ratio of 27 to 73 for the U.S. Army in fiscal 1975 and a ratio of 33 to 67 projected for fiscal 1977; this disparity narrows somewhat if combat formations in division support units and special mission units are counted as combat. A Soviet advantage is equally apparent vis-à-vis manpower within divisions allocated to maneuver battalions: 32 percent as opposed to only 23 percent for a U.S. division.[17] There is little doubt that the extraordinarily high ratio for the Soviet Army reflects heavy investment in initial combat power —in other words, preparation for a short, intense war—at the expense of the requisite support establishment to sustain a protracted conflict. The significance of the Soviet ratio for NATO's military forces, which are structured primarily for a longer war of less intensity, remains a contentious issue in the West.

Deployment Patterns

The current geographic distribution of Soviet divisions, set out in table 3-5, represents an extension of Russia's familiar "barbell" pattern of ground-force deployments. The bulk of those forces, including thirty-eight of the army's fifty tank divisions, is stationed west of the Ural Mountains, either in Eastern Europe or in European Russia. Southern Russia (the Caucasus and West Turkestan) and Central Russia (from the Urals to Lake Baikal) are thinly covered, but a second major concentration of

16. Assumes an average paper strength of 11,419 men per Soviet division— [(110 MRDs × 12,000) + (50 ADs × 9,500) + (7 AbDs × 7,000)]/167—and full manning levels for 56 divisions (56 × 11,419), 75 percent manning levels for 57 divisions (57 × 8,564), and 25 percent manning levels for 54 divisions (54 × 2,855). The number of active troops within Soviet Army divisions is thus 1,281,782— (56 × 11,419) + (57 × 8,564) + (54 × 2,855)—or 71.2 percent of a total active army manpower of 1.8 million.
17. Canby, *NATO Military Policy*, p. 13.

Table 3-5. Geographic Deployment of Soviet Army Divisions, by Type, 1974

Region	Motorized rifle	Armored	Airborne	Total
Eastern Europe	15	16	...	31
European Russia[a]	36	22	5	63
Southern Russia[b]	20	3	...	23
Central Russia[c]	4	1	...	5
Far East[d]	35	8	2	45
Total	110	50	7	167

Source: Author's calculations based on data appearing in *Military Balance, 1974–1975*, p. 9.
a. Russia west of the Urals.
b. Caucasus and West Turkestan.
c. Between the Urals and Lake Baikal.
d. Includes two Soviet divisions in Outer Mongolia.

Soviet forces is maintained in the Far East. The positioning of most Soviet divisions in the European area and along the Sino-Soviet border at the expense of garrisons in between the two regions reflects the traditional Russian fear of simultaneous conflict on two fronts—a fear undoubtedly heightened during the last fifteen years by the progressive deterioration of the USSR's relations with China. Indeed, as figure 3-1 demonstrates, the buildup of forces in the Far East represents the most dramatic change in the patterns of Soviet Army deployment since 1967.

Figure 3-1. Geographic Deployment of Soviet Army Divisions, 1967–74

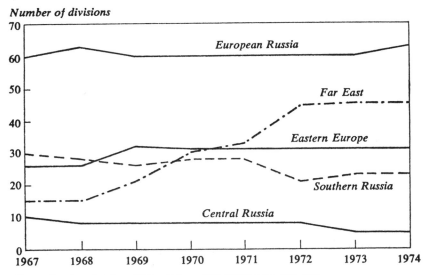

Source: Based on data from *Military Balance, 1965–1966* through *1974–1975*.

Table 3-6. Readiness of Soviet Army Divisions, by Category and Location, 1974

Location	Category I	Category II	Category III
Eastern Europe	31	...	...
European Russia	12	30	21
Southern Russia	3	10	10
Central Russia	...	...	5
Far East	10	17	18
Total	56	57	54

Source: Author's estimates based on information appearing in *Military Balance, 1974–1975.*

The precise character of the Far Eastern deployment is the subject of considerable debate. Some observers have interpreted the recent Soviet buildup as preliminary preparation for an invasion of Manchuria or a surgical strike designed to eliminate China's fledgling nuclear capabilities.

A close inspection of the structure of the deployment, however, leads to a different conclusion. First, according to at least one reputable source, the forty-five Soviet divisions now positioned in border areas simply match the number of People's Liberation Army divisions facing them,[18] a force ratio hardly conducive to major offensive operations on either side. The small number of armored divisions within the Soviet deployment also argues against a posture of attack; only 18 percent of the divisions are tank divisions, compared with 52 percent of the Soviet divisions in Eastern Europe. Even more persuasive is the lower readiness level of most Soviet divisions in the Far East (see table 3-6): only ten (22 percent) of the forty-five are maintained at full strength; the remaining thirty-five are kept in lower states of readiness, some even lacking a major portion of their authorized weapons and equipment. These factors, particularly when coupled with evidence that "a great deal of effort is going into the construction of barracks, accommodation for families, roads, rail spurs and permanent training grounds,"[19] strongly suggest a garrison force rather than a force poised for invasion. The offensive combat power of Far Eastern deployment, however, could be rapidly augmented should circumstances require.

In sharp contrast are the thirty-one combat-ready, full-strength, Russian divisions stationed in Eastern Europe—twenty in East Germany, two

18. "Will the Soviet Union Attack China?" *Strategic Survey 1973* (IISS, 1974), p. 67. The IISS defines the Sino-Soviet border area as the Soviet Trans-Baikal and Far Eastern Military Districts and Outer Mongolia; Chinese Sinkiang, Shenyung, and Peking Military Regions.

19. Ibid., p. 66.

in Poland, five in Czechoslovakia, and four in Hungary. Sixteen are armored divisions, a proportion that confers upon the deployment a distinct flavor of heavy investment in offensive strike capabilities. Twenty divisions (including ten armored), collectively designated the Group of Soviet Forces in Germany (GSFG), are maintained in East Germany. The GSFG is widely believed to represent the crème de la crème of the Soviet Army; no fewer than twelve of its divisions are "Guards" divisions,[20] whose elite status is reflected in higher pay and extra privileges. The amassing of such powerful military forces in East Germany—almost two-thirds of Russia's entire Eastern European deployment—suggests not only that the Soviets are concerned with maintaining stability in East Germany but also that the GSFG would be the cutting edge of any major thrust into NATO Center (Germany, minus Schleswig-Holstein, and the Benelux countries). The primary axis of advance, as suggested by the deployment pattern, is likely to be across the North German Plain or through the Fulda Gap. The terrain in those areas is better suited for swift armored penetration than is the more mountainous topography farther south; moreover, Soviet forces stationed in East Germany are closer to such key objectives as the Ruhr and the Channel ports than are Soviet or Pact divisions located elsewhere along the Central Front.

That the GSFG is structured principally for a massive blitzkrieg against Western Europe, regardless of the circumstances attending the outbreak of major hostilities on the Continent,[21] will become even more apparent in chapter 5, which reviews Soviet doctrine governing the use of its general-purpose forces in the European theater.

The question of whether the European and Far Eastern deployments are mutually supporting has long intrigued Western military analysts. Although the distance between the two "fronts" is some 6,000 to 8,000 miles, the Trans-Siberian Railway, as long as it remained intact, would

20. John Erickson, *Soviet Military Power* (London: Royal United Services Institute for Defense Studies, 1971), p. 36.

21. ". . . Whether a war between East and West in Europe were to be born of an offensive or a defensive Soviet politico-military policy, or was merely the unhappy offspring of an East-West misunderstanding, the result would be that the Warsaw Pact forces would immediately embark on the offensive and aim to defeat the NATO forces on the field of battle in a short, sharp, decisive campaign. . . . Such a war is indeed the only war that the Pact forces are equipped and trained to fight." P. H. Vigor and C. N. Donnelly, "The Soviet Threat to Europe," *Journal of the Royal United Services Institute for Defence Studies,* vol. 119 (March 1975); reprinted in U.S. Air Force, Current News Branch, *Current News* (29 April 1975), pp. 5–9 (the quotation appears on p. 5).

permit transfers of major forces from one theater to the other. During the first five months of the German invasion of Russia in 1941, eighteen fresh Soviet divisions were redeployed from the Far East to the Moscow area, where they proved instrumental in the successful defense of the Soviet capital.[22] And during the four months that preceded the Soviet invasion of Manchuria in August 1945, a total of 750,000 personnel, organized in thirty divisions and nine separate brigades, were transferred from the European theater to the Far East.[23] The success of these two redeployments, however, hinged upon the inability of the enemy to interdict the Trans-Siberian Railway, a condition that may not apply to future conflict. Moreover, for political as well as military reasons the USSR is highly unlikely completely to strip its European or Far Eastern garrisons to deal with pressure on another front.

Readiness and Mobilization Capabilities

A prominent characteristic of the Soviet Army is the staggered readiness of its divisions. Unlike U.S. ground forces, which are composed mostly of either units manned by active-duty personnel that are maintained at close to full strength or reserve units of "weekend warriors" requiring lengthy retraining to achieve combat effectiveness,[24] Soviet divisions fall into three categories of readiness, designed to permit massive, rapid, and uninterrupted mobilization. Category I divisions are units that are near full strength and are considered combat ready. There are an estimated fifty-six Category I divisions in the Soviet Army, most of them deployed in Eastern Europe and European Russia (see table 3-6). Category II divisions are believed deployable only following about thirty days of mobilization (M + 30). Although they are fully equipped, many of their fighting vehicles are kept in storage. Moreover, Category II divisions are manned at no more than 75 percent of their authorized strength and thus

22. Addington, *Blitzkrieg Era*, p. 208.

23. William Fowler, "Russia's War Against Japan," *Marshall Cavendish Illustrated Encyclopedia of World War II*, vol. 22 (Marshall Cavendish Corporation, 1972), p. 3000.

24. Martin Binkin, *U.S. Reserve Forces: The Problem of the Weekend Warrior* (Brookings Institution, 1974). As of 1975, the U.S. Army contains only one active division (the 2nd Infantry) with an affiliated reserve component. A second "active-reserve" division (the 7th Infantry) is to be added to the army by the end of fiscal 1977.

must be fleshed out with trained reservists before deployment. Category III divisions are essentially cadre formations containing only about 25 percent of their manpower and 50 percent of their equipment, most of which is stored. Judged deployable no sooner than M + 90, and more likely not until M + 120, even completely mobilized Category III divisions probably would be seriously deficient in first-line combat equipment and durable logistics-support vehicles because the remaining 50 percent of their equipment would have to be obtained from current production or from stockpiles of older and less reliable equipment.

In sum, it seems likely that by M + 60 the Soviet Army could completely mobilize *and* deploy up to 113 divisions (56 Category I and 57 Category II). By M + 120 it might be able to deploy its remaining 54 divisions, but these still would be deficient in equipment.[25]

In sharp contrast are U.S. mobilization plans, which for the most part continue to rely upon the time-consuming call-up and retraining of reserve units of much lower readiness. According to one estimate, National Guard divisions—the core of the U.S. reserve ground forces—would require a minimum of 100 to 180 days of retraining before they could become deployable as divisions, although individual reservists in those divisions could be used much earlier as fillers for active units. Long by Soviet standards, a period of 100 to 180 days still represents a vast improvement since World War II and the Korean War, when "it took a minimum of eleven months to ready these [Guard and Reserve] divisions for combat."[26]

The impressive speed with which the Soviet Army can mobilize and deploy very large forces to a potential theater of operations is illustrated in table 3-7 for three scenarios involving a war in NATO Center. *Scenario A* represents the most favorable circumstances for the USSR because the Soviet Union chooses to maximize its deployment opposite NATO Center in the shortest amount of time by (1) stripping its forces on its northern and southern flanks, (2) transferring one-third of its divisions in the Far East to the Central Front, and (3) creating by M + 60 an additional twelve divisions by amalgamating the active personnel and equipment of its Category III divisions in European Russia.

25. A more conservative estimate of Soviet mobilization capabilities appears in Thomas W. Wolfe, *Soviet Military Capabilities and Intentions in Europe,* P-5188 (RAND Corporation, March 1974), pp. 12–14.

26. "Report of the Secretary of Defense James R. Schlesinger to the Congress on the FY 1976 and Transition Budgets, FY 1977 Authorization Request and FY 1976–1980 Defense Programs" (February 5, 1975; processed), p. III-14. Hereafter, this document will be cited as "Report of the Secretary of Defense."

Table 3-7. Soviet Capacity to Mobilize and Deploy Divisions Opposite NATO
Center, M-Day through M + 120, Selected Scenarios, 1974

Date	Scenario A	Scenario B	Scenario C
M-Day[a]	27[b]	27[b]	27[b]
M + 7	31	31	31
M + 15	39	37	37
M + 30	59	55	55
M + 60	74	70	58
M + 90	79	70	58
M + 120	86	77	75

Sources: Author's estimates based on data appearing in Trevor N. Dupuy, John A. C. Andrews, and Grace P. Hayes, *The Almanac of World Military Power* (3rd ed., T. N. Dupuy Associates, 1974), pp. 160–61; Richard D. Lawrence and Jeffrey Record, *U.S. Force Structure in NATO: An Alternative* (Brookings Institution, 1974), pp. 18, 111–13; and *Military Balance, 1974–1975.* For conditions of the scenarios, see discussion in text.

a. The day on which mobilization begins.

b. All Soviet divisions now stationed in Eastern Europe with the exception of the four in Hungary, which are not considered deployable opposite NATO Center until M + 7.

Scenario B reflects the most likely pace of a Soviet buildup, in my view. While still combining some of its Category III divisions, the Soviet Army (1) deploys larger forces along the flanks at the expense of the Center, and (2) leaves its Far Eastern divisions undisturbed.

The distinguishing aspects of *Scenario C,* the least favorable circumstances for swift Soviet mobilization opposite NATO Center, are that (1) even larger forces are sent to the flanks, and (2) Category III divisions are not amalgamated but are deployed only by M + 120.

Arms and Equipment

The principal weapons of the Soviet Army are the tank, the surface-to-surface missile, and the artillery piece. Collectively, they represent the core of the army's conventional and nuclear firepower. The extent to which the Russians have organized their ground forces around these three weapons—forgoing other types of arms and equipment, particularly logistics support items (see chapter 4)—is unparalleled in any other modern army in the world. The devastating impact of Russian artillery barrages is legendary,[27] as is their inventory of tanks, currently estimated at over

27. The Red Army's final assault on Berlin in 1945 was initiated by a barrage delivered by 22,000 artillery pieces and heavy mortars. Edgar O'Ballance, *The Red Army: A Short History* (Praeger, 1964), p. 185.

40,000 units of widely varying types and quality.[28] An extraordinary emphasis on the surface-to-surface missile (SSM) for delivering munitions on the battlefield, evident in World War II in Soviet use of vast numbers of truck-mounted unguided rockets and the renowned multibarreled *Katyusha* rocket launcher, continues unabated. It is manifest in a panoply of similar weapons and in an inventory of no fewer than eight separate types of crew-served nuclear-capable SSMs. These include the FROG-2–7 series and the SCUD-A and SCUD-B.

The quality of Soviet arms is generally inferior to the best productions of the United States and its major NATO allies. Few would question the West's demonstrable technological lead in such areas as sophisticated avionics, fire-control systems, precision guidance, and certain types of ordnance; but until recently these technologies exercised less influence on the quality of ground forces than on the quality of air and naval forces. The latter are essentially capital-intensive forces whose continued military viability depends upon constant and costly technological innovation; land armies tend to be more labor-intensive forces, supported by fewer and less complex weapons.

Thus, the marked qualitative superiority that the West enjoys over the USSR with respect to tactical aircraft and strategic delivery systems traditionally has been less apparent in ground weapons. Indeed, Soviet artillery is generally considered superior to U.S. artillery—with respect to gun technology if not means of propulsion. The same may be true of armored personnel carriers. The new Russian BMP-76PB is widely rated as "among the finest APCs in the world";[29] it possesses an amphibious capability as well as the range and speed to keep up with fast-moving armored spearheads. Its design also permits troops to fire their weapons from within it while on the move, a capability denied to soldiers aboard the U.S. M-113 APC, who must dismount before engaging in combat. And while Soviet antitank missiles such as the wire-guided *Snapper, Swatter,* and *Sagger* are probably inferior to the U.S. *TOW* and *Dragon* systems, they proved a major obstacle to successful employment of armor by the Israelis during at least the opening phases of the October War of 1973.

A greater technological disparity between the USSR and NATO is evident in tanks. Although many of the basic characteristics of modern main

28. Dupuy and others, *Almanac of World Military Power,* p. 161; "Report of the Secretary of Defense," p. III-4.

29. R. E. Mattingly, "Defeating Soviet Armor," *Marine Corps Gazette,* vol. 59 (April 1975), p. 39.

Table 3-8. Selected Characteristics of First-Line Main Battle Tanks of Selected Countries

Characteristic	T-62 USSR	M-60A1 and A3[a] United States	Chieftain Mk. 5 Great Britain	Leopard I West Germany	AMX-30 France	S-Tank Sweden
Combat weight (tons)	40.2	53.0	62.0	44.3	39.6	43.0
Ratio of weight to horsepower	15.5:1	14.0:1	18.5:1	19.0:1	17.7:1	17.0:1
Maximum road speed (miles per hour)	30	30	30	40.5	40.3	31.1
Range (miles)	310[b]	310	310	375	400	250
Primary armament (millimeters)	115	105	120	105	105	105
Rounds carried	44	63	64	60	68	50
Maximum sustained rate of fire per minute	3–4	6	8[c]	6	8	15
Date of initial operational capability	1962	1962	1966	1965	1967	1968

Sources: *Comparative Characteristics of Main Battle Tanks* (Fort Knox, Kentucky: U.S. Army Armor School, June 1973; processed); and R. M. Ogorkiewicz, *S-Tank*, AFV/Weapons Profiles 28 (Profile Publications, 1971).

a. The A3 is scheduled for introduction into U.S. forces in 1976.

b. With integral fuel tanks; 445 with auxiliary fuel tanks.

c. Per first minute; 4 per minute thereafter.

battle tanks are remarkably similar, a notable difference is the lower rate of fire of the Soviet tanks and the smaller ammunition magazine for their primary armament (see table 3-8). Nor does the Soviet T-62 main battle tank compare well to NATO tanks in long-range gun accuracy and degree of armor protection. Additional weaknesses of the T-62 include terribly cramped crew space and dependence on dangerously exposed external fuel tanks for extended ranges. These factors explain in part the recurrent victories of Israeli-manned U.S. tanks over Egyptian-manned Soviet tanks in the October War, although the skills and leadership of tank crews certainly played an important role. These conclusions are supported by a recent assessment of the October War:

The T-62 proved to be robust and manoeuvrable, but the smooth bore of its gun precluded accuracy at the longer ranges. . . . The spin-stabilized armour-piercing rounds of the Israeli tank guns were at the outset able to pick off the Syrian attackers at ranges in excess of 2,000 metres. Then, as ranges lessened, the skill of the Israeli crews, combined with their tank-to-tank radios, which permitted warnings and target information to be exchanged, proved superior. Control within Syrian tank companies relied upon crude signals which were often misread. Accepting that the Syrian and Egyptian crews were less well trained than the Israelis—or than the tank corps of the Soviet Union—the T-62 did not manifest any particular advantage over the main battle tanks of Britain, the Federal Republic of Germany or the United States and was in many respects inferior, notably in having extremely vulnerable external fuel tanks.[30]

30. Elizabeth Monroe and A. H. Farrar-Hockley, *The Arab-Israeli War, October 1973: Background and Events,* Adelphi Papers 111 (IISS, 1975), p. 33.

On the other hand, Soviet tanks are much better prepared for combat in a chemical, biological, or radiological environment. Unlike U.S. and NATO tanks, Soviet tanks possess radiation-attenuating liners, special ventilation systems, and "automatic control units to seal the vehicle against blast effects and trigger the special ventilation system."[31]

As for future tank designs, the Soviet T-64, which is just now beginning to enter the inventory, appears to be little more than a modified T-62, whereas the XM-1, scheduled for delivery to the U.S. Army beginning around 1980, will possess a spectacular new type of armor said to be capable of withstanding the impact of any contemporary tank gun or anti-tank missile.

The most serious Soviet technological lag behind the West, however, lies in the development of precision-guided munitions, which promise to revolutionize the conduct of land warfare. Because of their high accuracy against exposed point targets, these weapons are thought not only to favor the defense—and thus to enhance NATO's conventional deterrent—but also to compromise severely the battlefield survivability of tanks and other armored fighting vehicles, upon which the Soviet Army has staked so much of its combat power.[32] Although the Soviets seem well-versed in wire-guided technologies, there are no indications of any proficiency in the more sophisticated realm of television- and laser-guided projectiles. The demonstrable U.S. lead in these areas was highlighted in 1972 by the use of laser- or television-guided—so-called smart—bombs in Indochina and in early 1975 by the Pentagon's announcement of successful test firings of a laser-guided artillery shell. Barring unforeseen technological hurdles, the so-called cannon-launched guided projectile, which is to be employed by the U.S. Army's hard-hitting 155-millimeter and 8-inch howitzers, could very well transform artillery from an indiscriminate area-fire weapon into a deadly enemy of individual tanks and other mobile-point targets.[33]

Yet the issue of quality must be placed in proper perspective: whatever the deficiencies of Soviet weapons in this regard, they may be more than

31. Steven Canby, *The Alliance and Europe, Part IV: Military Doctrine and Technology,* Adelphi Papers 109 (IISS, 1975), p. 4.

32. See, for example, Peter A. Wilson, "Battlefield Guided Weapons—the Big Equalizer," U.S. Naval Institute, *Proceedings,* vol. 101 (February 1975), pp. 19–25; and James F. Digby, "Precision-Guided Munitions: Capabilities and Consequences," Rand Paper Series 5257 (RAND Corporation, June 1974).

33. For an exposition of the potential impact of CLGPs on Soviet armor, see Canby, *Alliance and Europe.*

offset by quantity. Indeed, the Red Army (and before 1918, the Imperial Russian Army) has always emphasized numerical superiority as a key factor in success on the battlefield. During World War II, for example, while German production of medium tanks and assault guns was limited by the continual introduction and testing of fundamentally new designs— most of them superior to their predecessors and some even to Soviet models—the Soviet Union contented itself with simply modifying a few proven designs, most notably that of the renowned T-34. The result was that by the end of 1943, 18,000 medium tanks and assault guns were annually rolling off Soviet production lines compared with only 6,700 for Germany.[34]

Soviet emphasis on mass is no less evident today. According to one estimate, during the period 1972–74 the Russians out-produced the United States in tanks, APCs, and artillery pieces by average annual ratios of 6.5:1, 5:1, and 7:1, respectively.[35] And whereas in 1974 the nominal medium-tank strength in all active U.S. divisions and separate armored cavalry regiments, separate brigades, and special brigades totaled about 2,600,[36] medium tanks assigned to Soviet divisions alone numbered a staggering 30,700.[37] This gigantic inventory of armor is supplemented and supported by an estimated 30,000 armored personnel carriers, 12,000 artillery pieces ranging in size from 85 millimeters to 203 millimeters, 5,000 antitank guns, 4,000 truck-mounted 240-millimeter rocket launchers, 1,000 light antiaircraft guns, and a host of antitank, antiaircraft, and other missiles.[38]

These figures are subject to an important qualification, however: while about three out of every four Soviet tanks are assigned to divisions,[39] approximately 5,500 of the U.S. Army's present inventory of 8,200 tanks[40]

34. Seaton, *Russo-German War*, pp. 401–02.

35. "U.S./USSR Relative Production Rate Estimates," *Armed Forces Journal International*, vol. 112 (March 1975), p. 29.

36. Calculated on the basis of 44 armored battalions each with 54 medium tanks, and 15 armored cavalry battalions each with 17 tanks.

37. Assumes an average medium-tank strength per Soviet armored and motorized rifle division (airborne divisions have none) of 231—[(50 ADs × 325) + (110 MRDs × 188)]/160; and 50 percent tank strength (115) for 54 Category III divisions. Thus (106 × 231) + (54 × 115) = 30,696.

38. Dupuy and others, *Almanac of World Military Power*, p. 161.

39. Based upon a total Soviet inventory of medium tanks (T-62s and T-54/55s) estimated at 40,000 to 42,000.

40. The U.S. Army's authorized medium-tank strength in January 1975 was 10,000 units; however, due to a low rate of production (less than 50 units per month) and to large deliveries overseas (principally to Israel), the army registered a shortfall

are located outside combat units, mainly in war-reserve stockpiles abroad and in the United States, and in second sets of division equipment pre-positioned in Europe.

The disparity in the size of Soviet and U.S. tank inventories, both in the aggregate and within divisions, is also in part a function of differing approaches to the disposition of damaged equipment in wartime. In contrast to U.S. policy, which emphasizes repair of even heavily damaged items, Soviet policy calls for abandonment and replacement of crippled equipment. Although the Soviet approach reduces the logistics burden and thus enhances the army's ratio of combat to support troops, it does require larger inventories of equipment than a policy centering on retrieval.[41]

Other types of Soviet Army equipment are also plentiful. Notable items include an expanding inventory of troop- and cargo-carrying helicopters, and mobile bridges and bridge-laying paraphernalia mounted in tracked vehicles. Designed to facilitate the rapid crossing of water obstacles, Soviet bridging equipment demonstrated its effectiveness along the Suez Canal during the October War of 1973.

This abundance, however, does not extend to wheeled vehicles, which still form the backbone of a modern army's logistics capabilities. Indeed, it is in the realm of logistics support that the Soviets have paid most heavily in the opportunity costs of gearing their ground forces almost exclusively for short, armor-intensive conflict. For example, despite the fact that a much greater proportion of the logistics burden of the U.S. Army is borne by formations in the Initial Supporting Increments and Sustaining Supporting Increments *outside* the division, U.S. divisions nevertheless contain well over half again the number of trucks assigned to counterpart Soviet divisions (see table 3-9). Further proof of greater investment in organic staying power is the higher ratio of trucks to armored personnel carriers and tanks in U.S. divisions. The commercial vehicles and railways on which the Russians traditionally rely in wartime (see chapter 4), as

---

of about 1,800 tanks. For fiscal year 1976 the Defense Department has requested both a rise in the authorized inventory to 13,500 and funds to increase production of tanks in the M-60 series to 103 units per month. Large numbers of older M-48 tanks are also to be upgraded. "Report of the Secretary of Defense," pp. III-49–51.

41. The Russians take an analogous approach to combat units. Formations that sustain debilitating casualties are not to be reconstituted with individual fillers—the policy of the U.S. Army—but instead are to be replaced in their entirety by fresh units. The major advantages of the unit replacement system are that it eliminates the administrative overhead of processing each individual replacement separately and saves time in replacing large losses.

Table 3-9. Ratio of Trucks to Tanks and Armored Personnel Carriers in U.S. and Soviet Mechanized and Armored Divisions

Country and type of division	Trucks	Tanks and armored personnel carriers	Ratio of trucks to tanks and APCs
USSR			
Motorized rifle	1,350	496	2.7:1
Armored	1,300	515	2.5:1
United States			
Mechanized infantry	2,020	687	2.9:1
Armored	2,410	753	3.2:1

Sources: Author's calculations based on information appearing in Dupuy and others, *Almanac of World Military Power*, p. 160; "U.S. Army Armor Reference Data," vol. 1: "The Army Division" (Fort Knox, Kentucky: U.S. Army Armor School, 1974; processed); and "Infantry Reference Data," vols. 1 and 2 (Fort Benning, Georgia: U.S. Army Infantry School, 1972; processed).

was manifest in the invasion of Czechoslovakia in 1968, are no substitute for adequate wheeled transportation within an army; reliance on the civilian sector means dependence on scattered resources of varying utility. Moreover, the impact on nonmilitary transportation of the kind of war the USSR has planned for is likely to be devastating.

On the other hand, Soviet logistics capabilities are not incongruent with the kind of short, intense blitzkrieg that the Soviet Army is prepared to wage. Such a war might be short enough to obviate the need for comprehensive maintenance or replacement of armored forces. Furthermore, *blitzkrieg* tactics use armoured forces in such a way as to require relatively little logistic and indirect fire support. Large-scale fire and logistic support are required only during the heavy fighting of the initial breakthrough phase. Once a breakthrough occurs, an armoured penetration exploiting enemy disorganization requires relatively little artillery and logistic support. To provide all divisions and corps . . . with their own logistic capability for such infrequent occurrences as the breakthrough phase would be inefficient.[42]

Strategic Mobility

In sharp contrast to the United States, the ability of the USSR to project its military power on land beyond its traditional continental habitat is severely constrained by a limited strategic mobility. This is not surprising for a country that has never maintained large garrisons overseas, that is

42. Canby, *Alliance and Europe*, p. 10.

militarily allied with no state outside the Eurasian continent, and whose capacity to wage war is not dependent on the maintenance of transoceanic lines of communication. Indeed, small naval infantry forces, modest levels of amphibious shipping, and lack of carrier-based aviation all strongly suggest that the Soviet Navy is designed primarily not to project the

Soviet Union's power into distant oceans but to defend the security and interests of the USSR—by preventing attacks on its homeland and by limiting the role of the United States and other Western powers in regions close to Soviet shores. . . .[43]

Further, the growth of Soviet strategic airlift capability in recent years seems to be the result far less of a desire to project Soviet forces abroad than of the need for capacity to resupply munitions and equipment on short notice to beleaguered Soviet client states, particularly in the Middle East. In any event, armor-heavy Soviet motorized rifle and tank divisions are markedly ill-suited for swift and efficient airlift: the only Soviet transport aircraft capable of lifting medium tanks—the Antonov-22—can carry only two T-62s, and there are but thirty such aircraft estimated in the Air Transport Force.[44] Only the Soviet Army's airborne divisions could be airlifted with ease. Yet despite evidence that "strategic missions for . . . airborne troops have received increasing attention" in the USSR,[45] their very "lightness" probably would preclude their effective employment in combat environments dominated by armored operations or hostile air control, such as would be the case in the Middle East.

Ground Forces Allied to the USSR

No survey of Soviet Army capabilities, particularly in the crucial European area, is complete without a brief glance at East European ground forces. Unlike the North Atlantic Treaty Organization, the Warsaw Pact is an organization resting on enforced rather than voluntary loyalty; indeed, the bulk of Eastern European military forces may be regarded as an extension of Soviet military power on the Continent. Even in peacetime "for administrative, operational and logistical purposes the Warsaw Pact

43. Barry M. Blechman, *The Changing Soviet Navy* (Brookings Institution, 1973), p. 36.

44. The U.S. Military Airlift Command possesses seventy-nine C-5A heavy transports, each of which has a maximum payload capacity of 265,000 pounds compared with only 176,000 pounds for the Antonov-22.

45. Turbiville, "Soviet Airborne Troops," p. 64.

Table 3-10. Numbers of Men and Division Equivalents in Eastern European Ground Forces, by Country and Type of Division, 1974

Area and country	Total active army manpower (thousands)	Type of division[a]			
		Motorized rifle	Armored	Other[b]	Total
Northern Tier					
East Germany	145	4	2	...	6
Poland	220	8	5	2	15
Czechoslovakia	155	5	5	$\frac{1}{3}$	$10\frac{1}{3}$
Total, Northern Tier	520	17	12	$2\frac{2}{3}$	$31\frac{1}{3}$
Southern Tier					
Hungary	90	5	1	...	6
Rumania	141	8	2	$\frac{7}{9}$	$10\frac{7}{9}$
Bulgaria	120	8	$1\frac{2}{3}$	...	$9\frac{2}{3}$
Total, Southern Tier	351	21	$4\frac{2}{3}$	$\frac{7}{9}$	$26\frac{4}{9}$
Total, Warsaw Pact	871	38	$16\frac{2}{3}$	$3\frac{1}{9}$	$57\frac{7}{9}$

Source: Author's estimates based on data appearing in *Military Balance, 1974–1975*.
a. Includes divisions of varying strength and readiness.
b. Includes airborne, amphibious assault, artillery, and mountain formations.

is . . . run on the lines of a Soviet Military District and the military forces of the Pact organized as yet another 'arm' of the Soviet armed forces."[46]

Eastern European armies are a prominent element in the European military balance. Although structured along Soviet lines and supplied and equipped largely by the USSR, they are generally believed to be inferior to the Soviet Army in terms of readiness and quality of weapons and equipment. The active ground forces of non-Soviet Warsaw Pact countries collectively muster almost 900,000 personnel organized around fifty-eight division equivalents (see table 3-10).

The table also divides members of the Pact into two groupings—the Northern Tier, encompassing East Germany, Poland, and Czechoslovakia, and the Southern Tier states of Hungary, Rumania, and Bulgaria. Northern Tier states lie directly opposite NATO Center in the crucial North German Plain. Their proximity to opposing NATO forces strongly argues for viewing them as part of the Soviet order of battle in any major eruption of hostilities on the Continent. Strong Soviet forces also are maintained in all three Northern Tier countries. In contrast, two of the

46. Erickson, *Soviet Military Power*, pp. 103–04.

Table 3-11. Capacity of Soviet and Northern Tier States to Mobilize and Deploy Divisions Opposite NATO Center, M-Day[a] through M + 30, 1974

Country	M-Day	M + 7	M + 15	M + 30
USSR	27[b]	31	37	55
East Germany	6	6	6	6
Poland	2[c]	13	13	13
Czechoslovakia	10	10	10	12[d]
Total	45[e]	60	66	86

Sources: Author's estimates based on data appearing in Dupuy and others, *Almanac of World Military Power*, pp. 139–63; Lawrence and Record, *U.S. Force Structure in NATO*, pp. 18, 111–13; and *Military Balance, 1974–1975*.

a. The day on which mobilization begins.

b. All Soviet divisions in Eastern Europe except those in Hungary.

c. Assumes that only two Polish divisions are at full strength on M-Day, with the rest available by M + 7.

d. Assumes that Czechoslovakia's two cadre divisions are available by M + 30.

e. Assumes that all Category I divisions located in the Northern Tier are available for deployment on M-Day.

Southern Tier states, Rumania and Bulgaria, are free of a peacetime Soviet military presence, and the smaller, less well-equipped, and more distant armies of the three are of questionable reliability for other than purely defensive operations. Thus, the Southern Tier is highly unlikely to contribute more than token forces to a Soviet offensive against Western Europe. Nevertheless, as table 3-11 demonstrates, the addition of only Northern Tier armies to a Soviet buildup along the Central Front (see table 3-7) would substantially augment the Soviet threat to Western Europe. It is doubtful, however, that even these armies would remain politically reliable in a sustained offensive operation. All in all, the Eastern European countries are an uncertain asset to the USSR and might even prove a liability.

CHAPTER FOUR

DOCTRINE GOVERNING THE USE
OF GROUND FORCES

The magnitude, disposition, and structure of the Soviet Army clearly reflect willful preparation for massive, rapid offensive operations at the theater level in Europe. Although contrary postures elsewhere and the limited global "reach" of the army suggest a predominantly defensive orientation outside the Continent, any remaining doubts as to the army's "blitzkrieg" orientation vis-à-vis Europe are unlikely to survive investigation of Soviet doctrine governing the use of ground and other general-purpose forces, which is the purpose of this chapter. Because space does not permit detailed treatment of all aspects of Soviet theater doctrine, the discussion centers on what I believe are its most salient features as related to ground forces. These include the primacy of the offensive, the decisive role of nuclear weapons, the extraordinary emphasis on mass and surprise, and postulated rapid rates of advance.[1]

The Primacy of the Offensive

Perhaps the most striking and pervasive element of Soviet military doctrine is its unabashed adulation of the offensive. Soviet writers uniformly contend that "victory over an enemy is achieved only by a resolute at-

1. For this discussion, I have relied heavily on three major doctrinal treatises recently published in Moscow: A. A. Sidorenko, *The Offensive (A Soviet View)* (1970); V. Ye. Savkin, *The Basic Principles of Operational Art and Tactics* (1972); and N. A. Lomov, *Scientific-Technical Progress and the Revolution in Military Affairs* (1973), all translated and published under the auspices of the U.S. Air Force (Government Printing Office, 1973, 1974, and 1974, respectively). Taken together, these works, which are part of an ongoing series on Soviet military thought, constitute perhaps the most comprehensive statement to date of extant Soviet doctrine on theater warfare.

tack,"[2] and therefore deem "the offensive as the main type of combat actions of [Soviet] troops."[3] Defensive operations, although recognized as sometimes unavoidable, are "a forced and temporary form of combat actions" because "a side which only defends is inevitably doomed to defeat."[4] The celebration of the attack that permeates Soviet attitudes toward virtually all forms of combat cannot be overstated; it stems from the fundamental proposition that "in a just war which can only be waged by our state, Soviet military strategy will have a decisive, active, and offensive character."[5] Even defensive operations are to be characterized by continual and vigorous counterattacks whose ultimate purpose is "creating conditions for shifting of the defending troops to decisive offensive operations."[6]

The full significance of this extraordinary emphasis of the offensive is revealed by the goals assigned to it. The aim is not simply to beat back an intruding adversary or to clear enemy forces from vital border areas—objectives characteristic of other military establishments, such as NATO, that are oriented principally toward defense. On the contrary, *regardless* of the circumstances attending the outbreak of major hostilities in Europe involving the USSR,

only a decisive attack conducted at high tempos and to a great depth ensures total victory over the enemy. The goal of the attack lies in the total defeat of the defending enemy and capture of vital areas of his territory. This goal is achieved by destruction of means of mass destruction and the enemy's main groupings with nuclear weapons, the fire of other means, and also the forceful advance to a great depth of tank and motorized rifle troops inter-working with aviation and airborne landings, and the bold move to the flanks and rear of the enemy and destruction of him piecemeal.[7]

The achievement of such unlimited goals in the case of a conflict in the European area would entail nothing short of a giant blitzkrieg across NATO Center leading to the rapid occupation of West Germany, the Low Countries, and France.[8] Against China it would probably encompass a

2. Savkin, *Basic Principles*, p. 242.
3. Sidorenko, *Offensive*, p. 3.
4. Savkin, *Basic Principles*, pp. 242, 241–42.
5. Lomov, *Scientific-Technical Progress*, p. 135.
6. Savkin, *Basic Principles*, p. 249.
7. Ibid., p. 255.
8. Leon Gouré, Foy D. Kohler, and Mose L. Harvey, *The Role of Nuclear Forces in Current Soviet Strategy* (University of Miami, Center for Advanced International Studies, 1974), p. 69; and Richard D. Lawrence and Jeffrey Record, *U.S. Force Structure in NATO: An Alternative* (Brookings Institution, 1974), p. 11.

multipronged operation aimed at the swift envelopment and conquest of Manchuria, China's industrial heartland.[9] The likely axes of attack probably would be similar to those of the Russian invasion of the Japanese puppet state of Manchukuo in 1945.

The ambitious objectives specified for offensive operations are clearly reflected in Soviet expectations as to the character of those operations. In the Soviet view the principal attributes of the offensive are massive shock power and speed: the former, to crush the enemy's initial defenses; the latter, to prevent recovery so that the enemy can be beaten in detail. Speed would be vital to the USSR in a European campaign: a protracted conflict would grant NATO time to mobilize and bring to bear its ultimately greater but typically more dispersed and less ready forces against a Soviet Army that lacks the staying power of U.S. and European forces. The rapidity and violence anticipated for Soviet offensive operations are revealed in the following two passages:

The offensive starts by making nuclear strikes with tactical missiles and aviation for the purpose of destroying the means of mass destruction and defeating the basic enemy grouping on the axis of the main strike of advancing troops.

After the nuclear strikes, for neutralizing and destroying the enemy which has not been destroyed by the nuclear weapons on the front line and in tactical depth, preparatory firing and fire support of the advancing subunits will be carried out.[10]

Mobile operations and *manoeuvre* are, in the Soviet view, the concomitant of the use of nuclear weapons. The large sectors for deployment are reduced to the narrower attack frontages in order to maximise the conditions for overcoming enemy defenses, after which strong armoured forces will be loosed into the rear and the deep rear. The anticipated rate of advance is in the order of 70 miles in a 24-hour period, the emphasis is on high-speed attacks, speedy crossing of river lines, the employment of airborne and helicopter-borne forces ahead of the advance, efficient cross-country movement, fighting with open flanks and striking on by night as well as by day. The basic attack form will be 'off the march' (without prior concentration) and the 'meeting engagement' ... the accepted form of action, both of them high-speed manoeuvres.[11]

Tank formations supported by infantry aboard armored personnel car-

9. Douglas C. MacCaskill, "The Soviet Union's Second Front: Manchuria," *Marine Corps Gazette*, vol. 59 (January 1975), p. 25.

10. Lomov, *Scientific-Technical Progress*, p. 150.

11. John Erickson, *Soviet Military Power* (London: Royal United Services Institute for Defense Studies, 1971), p. 70.

riers are to advance swiftly *"into the depth of the enemy's defense through the breaches formed by nuclear weapons."*[12] Key objectives such as bridges and airfields that are beyond the immediate reach of armored forces are to be assaulted by airborne units and held until a linkup with attacking ground formations can be achieved. The role of the tank is believed crucial:

According to their combat characteristics, tanks are better able to withstand the effects of nuclear weapons, possess high cross-country ability and speed of movement off the roads, and are capable of accomplishing rapid maneuvers and delivering an attack to a great depth. They can also quickly cross zones of enemy radioactive contamination. With the fire from their guns and an armored blow, tanks are able to wipe from their path surviving remnants of resisting enemy troops, deliver forceful attacks against their flanks and rear, and move to a great depth without halting.

Advancing day and night without stopping, tank troops quickly will penetrate into the enemy's deep rear and lead the remaining forces of attacking troops behind them. In offensive operations, tank troops will be the force which will rush to the ultimate goals of the planned operations in the shortest time along routes laid by nuclear weapons. All this permits drawing the conclusion that it is the tanks which can most effectively take advantage of the results of friendly nuclear strikes.[13]

No less important is the requirement to maintain the momentum of the offensive, reflected in the unparalleled emphasis on and preparation for river-crossing and night operations.[14] The Soviet view holds that "daylight attacks are connected with tremendous losses";[15] moreover, refusal to press the offensive at night not only slows the advance and permits the enemy to redeploy but also deprives attacking forces of darkness to conceal their movements and thereby reduce the likelihood of being targeted by enemy nuclear and tactical aviation strikes.

In sum, the principal role assigned to ground forces under Soviet theater doctrine is one of relentless attack, "blitzkrieg style," designed to ensure the *total* defeat of the enemy and the occupation of vital territory. This extraordinary doctrinal attention to offensive operations that are virtually unlimited in scope would be less disturbing to potential adversaries of the USSR were it not for two factors. First, acclaim of the offensive contradicts Soviet diplomatic claims that the purpose of their military forces— for example, the Soviet Army's thirty-one full-strength divisions in Eastern

12. Sidorenko, *Offensive,* p. 62; italics in the original.
13. Savkin, *Basic Principles,* p. 195.
14. Ibid., p. 257; and Sidorenko, *Offensive,* pp. 200–20.
15. Ibid., p. 35.

Europe—is a purely protective one geared to the preservation of the territorial integrity of the USSR and its allies. The complete destruction of an enemy's armed forces and the conquest of its homeland can hardly be subsumed under the rubric of simple self-defense. Second, unlike other military establishments that have worshiped the offensive, the Soviet Army, as demonstrated in chapter 3, appears eminently capable of responding to the demands of its doctrine. This consistency between Soviet doctrine and ground-force structure stands in sharp contrast, for example, to the inconsistency that characterized the French Army before 1914, which genuflected before the Napoleonic altar of audacious attack while lacking adequate large-caliber artillery and taking a generally defensive posture.

The Decisiveness of Nuclear Weapons

Even before U.S. strategic forces reached their present murderous level of capability, common sense suggested that the USSR would be chary of initiating use of tactical nuclear weapons, given the risk of strategic escalation. Yet most published Soviet doctrinal treatises continue to maintain that "nuclear weapons [are] the basic means of destruction on the field of battle"[16]—more specifically, that the "strategic and tactical missile forces are the basis of the firepower of the Land Forces for defeating the enemy."[17] Indeed, it is the employment of nuclear weapons—principally nuclear surface-to-surface missiles—that allows the most rapid realization of Soviet ambitions with respect to offensive operations, although success by nonnuclear means is not excluded:

Nuclear weapons are the most powerful means for the mass destruction of troops and rear area objectives. Among all other means of combat, they possess the greatest force for physical and moral-psychological influence and therefore they have decisive influence on the nature of the offensive. During the entire history of military art, no one weapon had such sudden and rapid influence on the nature of the offensive and on the conflict as a whole as did nuclear weapons. Their employment in the battle and operation permits inflicting large losses in personnel and equipment on the enemy almost instantaneously, destroying, paralyzing and putting out of action entire [regiments, divisions], and even [corps], and thereby changing the relation of forces sharply in one's favor and destroying structures and other objectives as well as enemy centers of resis-

16. Ibid., p. 41.
17. Lomov, *Scientific-Technical Progress*, pp. 105–06.

tance and frustrating his counterattacks and counterblows. Thanks to this, the troops can conduct the offensive at high rates and achieve the assigned goals in short times.[18]

However, the decisive role formally imputed to nuclear arms by Soviet doctrine is attenuated somewhat by recent Soviet writings and war games. They have (1) indicated a growing acceptance of the possibility that a war in Europe might have an initial conventional phase—a principal focus of NATO strategy and force planning since the adoption of flexible response in 1967—and (2) emphasized that Soviet "forces must be prepared to fight without using nuclear weapons, utilizing the standard conventional 'classical' weapons."[19] This is in contrast to an earlier judgment that the

prospect that belligerents might confine themselves to conventional warfare in any large-scale conflict does not seem to be entertained in . . . Soviet doctrine, even though the Soviet military establishment continues to maintain a dual capability for both conventional and nuclear warfare. One of the more striking aspects of the doctrine is its almost exclusive concentration on nuclear warfare.[20]

In sum, Soviet doctrine appears progressively to have backed away from the notion that the use of nuclear weapons in any large war in Europe would be *inevitable,* although Soviet writers still believe it *highly probable.*

Another recent change in Soviet doctrine relates to whether a major conflict characterized by combat directly between Soviet and U.S. or Chinese forces would inevitably lead to a *strategic* nuclear exchange. Although throughout the 1950s and early 1960s Soviet writers resolutely contended that "there is no difference in the tactical and strategic use of atomic weapons,"[21] doctrinal pronouncements since then have suggested acceptance of an escalatory watershed separating theater (tactical) and strategic employment of nuclear weapons.

On the other hand, there are no indications that the Russians now view theater nuclear war (that is, theater use of nuclear weapons), should

18. Sidorenko, *Offensive,* p. 40.

19. Marshal I. I. Yakubovsky, "Soviet Ground Forces," *Red Star* (July 21, 1967); reprinted in abridged form in *Survival,* vol. 9 (October 1967), p. 327.

20. V. D. Sokolovskii, ed., *Soviet Military Strategy* (Military Publishing House of the Ministry of Defense of the USSR, 1962), translated and with an analytical introduction, annotations and supplementary material by Herbert S. Dinerstein, Leon Gouré, and Thomas W. Wolfe (a RAND Corporation Research Study; Prentice-Hall, 1963), pp. 50–51.

21. N. Talenskii, "About Atomic and Conventional Weapons," *Mezkdunarodnaia zhizń* (*International Affairs*) (January 1955), p. 25.

it occur, as divisible into gradations of violence or limitable geographically. Indeed, the controlled and selective use of theater nuclear weapons for demonstrative or political signaling purposes—the core of NATO's flexible-response strategy—is the subject of derision in Soviet doctrine,[22] which, as noted above, stresses the war-fighting capabilities of theater nuclear weapons and not their deterrent value. On the contrary, Soviet military strategy, at least in Europe, calls for the "mass employment of nuclear weapons"[23] once the nuclear threshold has been crossed. Emphasis on massive (and therefore comparatively indiscriminate) use of tactical nuclear weapons (TNW) certainly represents no departure from the seemingly ageless tradition of the Russian military, which has never accentuated "pinpoint accuracy and strict target selection but rather mass barrages intended to smash paths through enemy formations and rear areas for the ground units to exploit."[24] It may also be in part a function of the character of the Soviet inventory of such weapons. Generally larger in yield and less accurate than NATO's,[25] Soviet TNW in fact raise the question of whether the USSR could wage a limited, selective theater nuclear war even if it so desired.

In short, should a future conflict with the USSR's principal adversaries escalate beyond conventional combat, Soviet doctrine attaches decisive importance to massive use of nuclear arms even in a war that did not directly disturb the homelands of the major protagonists. In such a conflict the main responsibilities of the Soviet Army, which is the primary repository of Soviet theater TNW capabilities, would be the delivery of nuclear strikes and their exploitation. However, this does not remove the need for sizable ground forces, because

it cannot be imagined that in a nuclear war, even in the main theaters of military actions, all the missions will be carried out with just nuclear missile weapons. It is advisable and advantageous to carry out a whole series of missions with conventional weapons (for example, neutralizing many military targets on the battlefield, capturing enemy territory, and so forth).[26]

A sizable ground force is also necessary as a hedge against prolonged

22. Gouré and others, *Role of Nuclear Forces*, p. 111.
23. Sidorenko, *Offensive*, pp. 58, 61.
24. Martin J. Miller, Jr., "Soviet Nuclear Tactics," *Ordnance*, vol. 14 (May–June 1970), p. 627.
25. For a more detailed description of the character of Soviet TNW and the doctrine governing their use, see Jeffrey Record, *U.S. Nuclear Weapons in Europe: Issues and Alternatives* (Brookings Institution, 1974), chap. 5.
26. Lomov, *Scientific-Technical Progress*, p. 73.

conflict that, contrary to expectations, did not cross the nuclear threshold. Indeed, growing Soviet attention to nonnuclear combat is encouraging in light of the dubious usefulness of a nuclear-oriented strategy of theater warfare. One of the most disquieting aspects of Soviet doctrine is its implication that something called "victory" could emerge from a full-scale theater nuclear war. The term presumably refers to the destruction of enemy forces and occupation of vital areas of territory. However, "mass employment of nuclear weapons" as the preferred means of realizing those objectives almost certainly would entail enormous civilian and military casualties as well as the utter ruin of much, if not most, of the territory to be occupied. Also not to be discounted is the probable transformation of large areas into radioactive "deserts" incapable of supporting human or plant life.

This judgment appears eminently realistic with respect to densely populated Europe, where an estimated 2,250 Soviet TNW confront a NATO deployment of some 7,000. Even a massive employment of Soviet TNW that did not provoke a nuclear response from NATO would deprive Europe of any industrial or agricultural value that might otherwise accrue to the USSR. Over two-thirds of Soviet TNW are believed to possess yields well in excess of the 13-kiloton Hiroshima bomb; more than 500 contain yields ranging from ½ to 3 megatons.[27] Mutual use—the more likely contingency, given current NATO strategy and the difficulties involved in any attempt to destroy NATO's massive and multifarious tactical nuclear deployment in a first strike—would only increase the magnitude of devastation. The probability of holocaust is supported by results of war games and studies undertaken by the Department of Defense in the 1960s, which showed that

high casualty rates and a great amount of collateral damage were likely to result from a tactical nuclear war in Europe. Even under the most favorable assumptions, it appeared that between 2 and 20 million Europeans would be killed, with widespread damage to the economy of the affected area and a high risk of 100 million dead if the war escalated to attacks on cities.[28]

Nor could Soviet ground formations and rear areas in Eastern Europe hope to evade staggering losses and severe disruption since both would be prime targets of NATO's more numerous and comparatively accurate TNW.

27. Record, *U.S. Nuclear Weapons in Europe*, p. 38.
28. Alain C. Enthoven and K. Wayne Smith, *How Much Is Enough? Shaping the Defense Program, 1961–1969* (Harper and Row, 1971), p. 128.

In sum, aside from drastically increasing the risk of a strategic exchange, a Soviet resort to "mass employment of nuclear weapons" at the theater level would appear to be self-defeating. An offensive that ended with the occupation of a devastated and contaminated Western Europe by remnants of a gutted Soviet Army could hardly be called a "victory."

The Continuing Importance of Mass

Large ground forces are further justified because nuclear combat "will lead to *mass losses of troops and equipment"* that can be absorbed only by forces that are themselves massive.[29] Thus, traditional Russian emphasis on the sheer weight of numbers as a key to success in war has survived into the nuclear era despite the enormous energy and resources that have been devoted to qualitative improvement of Soviet arms since the death of Stalin. Soviet investment in numerical superiority is unmistakably evident in the size of the Red Army and in the vast quantities of major items of equipment such as tanks, artillery, and aircraft that are maintained in active inventories. All are designed to enhance shock power and to guarantee the Soviet military not only an overall preponderance of forces but also a superiority at the tactical level.

Because one of the opportunity costs of investment in numbers is an otherwise faster pace of modernization, one wonders why the USSR maintains such a large military establishment in an era when most developed countries have opted for smaller but technologically more proficient forces. Among the many probable explanations is the search for compensation for precisely that enduring (and to date well-founded) sense of technological inferiority vis-à-vis the West. Beyond that is Soviet experience during the Great Patriotic War, which, according to one prominent Soviet military writer, proved "that superiority in number of troops always acted as one of the most important premises for victory over the enemy."[30] Indeed, Soviet doctrinal literature is replete with detailed force-ratio and troop-density analyses drawn from the Second World War that are offered as evidence to support continuing emphasis on quantitative preponderance.

29. Sidorenko, *Offensive,* p. 61.
30. Savkin, *Basic Principles,* p. 91.

The Enhanced Value of Surprise

As a country that has experienced the horrendous consequences of a
surprise invasion and that is determined "never again [to] allow itself to
be caught unawares and [to] permit the enemy to hold the initiative,"[31]
the Soviet Union attaches great importance to achieving both strategic
and tactical surprise in future combat. Surprise is an age-old principle of
warfare; current Soviet doctrine, however, contends that the advent of
"nuclear weapons has considerably increased the role and importance of
surprise"[32] because

> delay in the destruction of [the enemy's] means of nuclear attack will permit
> the enemy to launch . . . nuclear strikes first and may lead to heavy losses and
> even to the defeat of the offensive. The accumulation of such targets as nuclear
> weapons and waiting with the intention of destroying them subsequently are
> now absolutely inadmissible.[33]

Although the issue of surprise attack is formally treated as a threat *to*
the Soviet Union—the USSR never starts wars but only responds to conflict imposed upon it by imperialist enemies—the extensive, public attention it receives in Soviet military literature strongly suggests great interest
in a *Soviet* strategy based on surprise. Indeed, the advantages attributed
to surprise attack indicate a firm belief that a military establishment that
refused to strike first would be derelict in its responsibilities toward its
homeland.

In fact, some statements bearing on Soviet doctrine do not make a clear
distinction between surprise and preemption. For example, "the side
which first employs nuclear weapons with surprise can predetermine the
outcome of the battle in his favor";[34] "surprise blitzkriegs with nuclear
weapons, aviation, and tank groupings may be irresistible";[35] and "preemption in launching a nuclear strike is . . . the decisive condition for the
attainment of superiority over [the enemy] and the seizure and retention
of the initiative."[36] A Radio Moscow broadcast in 1970, after dismissing
the idea that the USSR would ever fall victim to the kind of protracted

31. Gouré and others, *Role of Nuclear Forces,* p. 107.
32. Savkin, *Basic Principles,* p. 230.
33. Sidorenko, *Offensive,* p. 134.
34. Ibid., p. 112.
35. Savkin, *Basic Principles,* p. 232.
36. Sidorenko, *Offensive,* p. 115.

conventional war preferred by Chinese military doctrine, went on to conclude that

in a nuclear war an enemy can deal very powerful nuclear strikes on the most densely populated areas of a target country at the outbreak of the war without sending troops to invade it. Can this [that is, Chinese] military theory based on a defensive and deceptive action to lead an enemy into an unfavorable position provide any answer to such military operations by the enemy? No, it cannot.[37]

Thus, along with its sister forces, the Soviet Army appears to be doctrinally propelled toward operations that not only are offensive in orientation but have as their major aim the prevention of an effective military response on the part of potential adversaries through preemptive attack.

Postulated Rapid Rates of Advance

The fearsomeness of Soviet offensive operations is bolstered by the stunning rate of advance postulated for armored and motorized rifle formations that are to be the cutting edge of the advance. A sustained advance averaging no less than approximately *70 miles per day* is deemed the minimum required to fulfill the ambitious goals of offensive operations discussed above.[38] In Europe such a pace would bring Soviet forces to the Rhine in less than 48 hours and to the Channel ports within a week; against China it would mean a lightning penetration in depth and an envelopment of Manchuria before Chinese forces could organize an effective territorial defense.

However, there are a number of reasons for suspecting that the Soviet Army might fall short of fulfilling this particularly ambitious tenet of its doctrine. First, a sustained rate of advance of 70 miles a day would be quite unprecedented, at least in the European theater. As shown in table 4-1, five highly acclaimed armored campaigns on the Continent during the Second World War—including Guderian's famous "race to the sea" in

---

37. Quoted in Gouré and others, *Role of Nuclear Forces*, p. 31.

38. Malcolm Mackintosh states that Soviet "ground force operations are expected to take place at very high speeds, up to seventy-five miles a day across open country"; *Juggernaut: A History of the Soviet Armed Forces* (Macmillan, 1967), p. 306. In another assessment, Trevor Cliffe concludes that the Russians expect their armored forces "to advance at an average rate of 60 miles a day or even more, negotiating river crossings with a minimum of delay and continuing the offensive by night as well as by day"; *Military Technology and the European Balance,* Adelphi Papers 89 (IISS, 1972), p. 33. See also Erickson, *Soviet Military Power,* p. 70.

Table 4-1. **Rates of Advance for Selected Campaigns during the Second World War**

Date	Area of operation	Unit	Depth of operation (miles)	Duration (days)	Average daily rate of advance (miles)
May–June 1940	Northern France and Low Countries	German XIXth Army Corps (Guderian)	300	25	12.0
June 1941	Western Russia	German 2nd Panzer Group (Guderian)	200	6	33.3
November 1942	Volga Basin	Soviet 5th Tank Army	87	5	17.4
August 1944	Yassy and Kishinev	Soviet 6th Tank Army	400	8	50.0
August 1944	Northern France	U.S. 3rd Army (Patton)	255	22	12.1
August 1945	Manchuria	Soviet 6th Guards Tank Army	510	10	51.0

Sources: Jeffrey Record, "Armored Advance Rates: A Historical Inquiry," *Military Review*, vol. 53 (September 1973), pp. 63–72; John F. Sloan, "Soviet Armed Forces," *Military Review*, vol. 55 (January 1975), p. 112; and William Fowler, "Russia's War Against Japan," *Marshall Cavendish Illustrated History of World War II*, vol. 22 (Marshall Cavendish Corporation, 1972), pp. 2997–3009.

1940 and Patton's celebrated thrust across northern France in 1944—registered daily gains averaging substantially less than that now postulated for Soviet ground forces. Moreover, in none of the campaigns listed in the table did advancing forces encounter more than relatively light resistance, the principal factor governing rates of advance.[39] This was certainly the case with respect to much of the Soviet campaign in Manchuria in 1945, often cited in Soviet doctrinal literature as a model for future offensive operations. Because of a staggering Soviet preponderance over the crumbling Japanese Kwantung Army,[40] the progress of many Soviet formations was facilitated by the absence of *any* resistance, as was the case with the 6th Guards Tank Army during the first four days of its celebrated campaign.[41]

Although postwar armored campaigns in the Middle East have achieved higher rates of advance—again, due in most instances to ineffective resistance—the vast expanses of treeless, desert terrain characteristic of the Sinai peninsula differ sharply from the wooded, river-laced topography of Central Europe. Furthermore, as was demonstrated on the Sinai front

39. Jeffrey Record, "Armored Advance Rates: A Historical Inquiry," *Military Review,* vol. 53 (September 1973), pp. 63–72.

40. The Soviet-Japanese numerical balance of forces in the Far East on the eve of the Manchurian campaign was approximately as follows: divisions—3.3:1; independent brigades—4.2:1; armored vehicles (including tanks)—4.5:1; artillery and mortars—3.9:1; aircraft—3:1. Moreover, the bulk of Japanese arms and equipment was pathetically obsolete and most Japanese divisions were woefully understrength.

41. William Fowler, "Russia's War Against Japan," *Marshall Cavendish Illustrated History of World War II,* vol. 22 (Marshall Cavendish Corporation, 1972), p. 3004.

during the Yom Kippur War in 1973, even Israel's renowned tank formations could be stopped cold by properly organized defenses.

Historical precedent, however, is often violated. Thus, a more important constraint is the questionable ability of the Soviet logistics infrastructure to support a pace of 70 miles a day. Indeed, as pointed out earlier, a major penalty of the Soviet's one-sided investment in initial shock power and combat capabilities (that is, in the "short-war" option) has been a limited ability to sustain such forces in combat over an extended period. Soviet logistics-support capabilities are markedly inferior to those of the United States and other Western military establishments (see chapter 4), which devote far greater attention to preparation for protracted conflict. For example, unlike NATO forces, the Soviet Army—in part because of insufficient organic wheeled transport—is dependent principally on railroads for transporting men and supplies to the front. A Soviet field army (three to five divisions) normally operates from 60 to 95 miles of its own railhead, which in turn serves a number of depots within about 20 miles of the front. Each depot supports up to three divisions through a road network; trucks thus link the depots to the front. According to Soviet doctrine, as the front advances rail lines are extended and railheads and depots relocated forward.

At least three weaknesses are apparent in the "railhead" method of supporting front-line combat formations, which is a legacy of Soviet logistics organization during the Second World War. First, the mobility of modern armored forces promises to advance the front at a pace much faster than that at which railheads and depots could be extended to support it, especially if a retreating enemy has destroyed rail facilities in the territory about to be occupied. The result would be a heavier burden on road-bound transport, in which the Soviet Army is notoriously deficient.

A second problem is that rail lines are more exposed than roads to interdiction by tactical air and guerrilla forces and require a longer time to repair. No better example of this greater vulnerability exists than the near-paralysis of the German rail network in the Soviet Union inflicted by Russian partisans during the Second World War, in contrast to their less successful attempts to block road-bound traffic. Although units of troops specializing in railroad repair are maintained by the Soviet Ministry of Defense, they do not appear to be capable of rebuilding daily anything close to 70 miles of damaged or destroyed tracks, roadbeds, and bridges.

Finally, the gauge of Soviet railroads is broader than that of European railroads. This difference complicates and delays the movement of forces from Russia's western military districts into Eastern Europe, a key element in Russia's ability to increase its military power along the Central Front.[42]

These and other deficiencies in Soviet logistics support were amply exposed during the invasion of Czechoslovakia in 1968. Despite the absence of armed resistance, advancing Soviet armor quickly outran its rail-based supply depots, and there were not enough trucks and other logistics-support vehicles to constitute an adequate substitute. As a result,

during the first week of the occupation . . . a breakdown of transportation and supply services threatened to paralyze the Soviet armies in Czechoslovakia [and] the situation was saved by . . . [an] airlift which delivered fuel, food, and essential equipment. . . . Under actual combat conditions . . . [Soviet divisions] would have lacked many essential items after the first 24 hours.[43]

42. During the Second World War the Germans encountered the same obstacle, but in reverse. Troops and supplies headed for the Eastern Front by rail had to be transferred at the Soviet-Polish border onto Russian trains—the only ones suited to Soviet railroads. The resulting delays were exacerbated when the retreating Russian forces destroyed much of their own rolling stock.

43. Leo Heiman, "Soviet Invasion Weaknesses," *Military Review,* vol. 49 (August 1969), pp. 42, 43.

CHAPTER FIVE

CONCLUSIONS

The foregoing analysis has revealed the Soviet Army to be a large, powerful military establishment oriented mainly toward Europe and structured primarily for a short, intense war characterized by massive high-speed offensive operations designed to overwhelm its opponents. Conclusive evidence of this posture is manifest in the Soviet Army's size and disposition, its heavy investment in armor, its unsurpassed degree of mechanization, and its impressive mobilization capacity.

Preparation for blitzkrieg also is conspicuous in Soviet doctrine governing the use of ground forces. Among the principal tenets of that doctrine are the supremacy of offensive operations, the decisiveness of nuclear arms, the continued importance of numerical advantage, the heightened value of surprise—indeed, preemption—and the designation of unparalleled rates of advance for attacking formations. All of these propositions derive from a fundamental assumption on the part of the Russians that any major conflict in Europe between the USSR and NATO probably would encompass an early use of nuclear weapons, and certainly the ever-present threat of their use.

Yet the placement of so many "eggs" in the short-war "basket" has not been without its price. Whatever the combat prowess of the Soviet Army, its ability to exercise it beyond Russia's traditional continental habitat is severely constrained by limited strategic mobility resources. Moreover, emphasis on initial shock and firepower has come at the expense of an ability to maintain intense levels of combat in a war whose duration exceeded Soviet expectations.

Often cited as evidence of Soviet recognition of these weaknesses is growing Soviet attention in recent years to logistics support and strategic airlift. The new concern, however, probably represents a desire to enhance existing capacity to sustain a short war rather than a fundamental reorientation toward protracted conflict. For the foreseeable future the Soviet Army will be denied the ability to wage for a prolonged period the kind of intense offensive operations envisioned in present doctrine. Such a judgment, of course, would not apply to defensive operations conducted in Eastern Europe or on Soviet territory.

Of greater significance is the modest but progressive erosion of Soviet fixation on nuclear weapons as the preferred and only decisive means of waging a theater war in Europe. The dramatic upgrading and expansion of Soviet conventional forces in the European area during the first half of the 1970s, as well as recent doctrinal pronouncements and war games, suggest a much less rigid approach to the subject than in the past. This apparent reassessment of the role of nuclear weapons could lead to greater Soviet interest in precision-guidance technologies, an area in which the present Soviet lag behind the West promises to impose major penalties upon Soviet offensive operations at the conventional level.

As for the future, there is little reason to anticipate any fundamental alteration of the Soviet Army's posture in the European area. That posture takes full advantage of both the decided numerical superiority of the Warsaw Pact in active combat forces in the region and the highly favorable geographical position of the Soviet Union vis-à-vis the United States. Sizable Soviet ground forces geared principally for a theater-wide offensive are likely to be retained indefinitely in Eastern Europe, barring an improbable major breakthrough at the Vienna talks on mutual and balanced force reduction. Only a requirement for another substantial buildup in the Far East could conceivably result in a depletion of Soviet forces in Europe; however, to date, augmentation of forces in that region has been achieved without disturbing deployments on the USSR's primary front.

Nor is there likely to be a change in Soviet reliance on tanks supported by mechanized infantry as the core of the army's shock and initial striking power. The debate in Western military circles that followed the Yom Kippur War over the viability of armor in a battlefield environment dominated by precision-guided munitions has had no visible parallel in the USSR, although growing Soviet investment in tactical air defense weapons does suggest heightened concern over the NATO air threat to Soviet armor.

The implications of the Soviet Army's "short war" posture for the size and structure of NATO forces were discussed in detail in one of my earlier works.[1] That study's recommendations for restructuring U.S. forces to

1. See Richard D. Lawrence and Jeffrey Record, *U.S. Force Structure in NATO: An Alternative* (Brookings Institution, 1974).

deal more effectively with the specific Soviet threat in Europe included (1) increasing the ratio of combat to support troops within the U.S. Seventh Army; (2) speeding up the rate at which U.S. forces in the United States could be deployed to Europe; (3) reorienting U.S. tactical aviation on the Continent away from air superiority-deep interdiction and toward close air support; and (4) redeploying major U.S. ground combat forces northward astride the likely avenues of a Soviet invasion. The ability to counter a Soviet blitzkrieg would be further enhanced by the mechanization of more of the U.S. Army's infantry divisions. With these recommendations in mind, and given the recent and continuing strengthening of Soviet ground forces in Europe, proposals for reducing NATO combat forces appear singularly ill-timed, to say the least. Qualitative NATO superiority in ground combat equipment and, more important, in tactical air power may well compensate for the present Soviet quantitative advantage in ground forces; but it would be imprudent to believe that the resulting balance could be maintained indefinitely if NATO further reduces its combat forces in the European theater in the face of the strengthening of Soviet forces. An attempt to evade resulting hard choices by relying on selective NATO use of tactical nuclear weapons has little to commend it in view of the evident Soviet belief that any tactical nuclear exchange would quickly assume massive proportions.

Admittedly, my analysis of Soviet ground forces does not *automatically* lead to firm conclusions regarding the size and structure of U.S. and allied forces; many other factors are involved, including a judgment as to the chances of war in Europe, which now seem very low. Nonetheless, any prescription for U.S. and allied general purpose forces that does not take into explicit account the specific character of the Red Army rests on very shaky intellectual ground.

A Note on Soviet Tactical Aviation

No assessment of Soviet ground-warfare capabilities can exclude a brief look at the potential contribution of Soviet tactical aviation to the land battle, since the interaction between air and ground forces is crucial in modern combat. My purpose here is simply to identify the basic features of the Soviet tactical air force; more detailed analyses are plentiful and should be consulted by readers desirous of further information.[1]

Unlike U.S. and Western European tactical air forces, Soviet aviation is not oriented principally toward achieving air superiority and the interdiction of logistical, military, and economic targets well behind enemy lines. Nor is it, like the German Luftwaffe of World War II, designed mainly to provide close support for engaged ground forces. On balance, Soviet aircraft do not possess the range, payload, durability, or sophisticated avionics that are characteristic of aircraft optimized for air superiority-deep interdiction; their limited payload and loiter time also render them comparatively inefficient in the ground-attack role.

The primary focus of Soviet tactical aviation is rather upon strategic and tactical air defense, a not surprising concomitant of deliberate concentration of conventional military strike power in ground forces. Emphasis on air defense at the expense of other missions is apparent in the organization of nearly 3,000 interceptors—over 40 percent of the USSR's estimated total inventory of almost 7,000 tactical combat aircraft[2]—into the Air Defense Command, a military service separate from the Soviet Air Forces. A large portion of the remaining 4,000 aircraft are configured mainly for achieving local air superiority; only 2,800 are subsumable

1. See, for example, William F. Scott, "Soviet Aerospace Forces and Doctrine," *Air Force Magazine,* vol. 58 (March 1975), pp. 33–43; and R. Meller, "Europe's New Generation of Combat Aircraft: Part 1: The increasing threat," *International Defense Review,* vol. 8 (April 1975), pp. 175–86.

2. William D. White, *U.S. Tactical Air Power: Missions, Forces, and Costs* (Brookings Institution, 1974), p. 112.

Table A-1. Tactical and Strategic Defense Air Assets of NATO and Warsaw Pact Members, by Number of Aircraft Assigned to Operating Squadrons and Designated Mission, Fiscal Year 1974

Alliance and member	Tactical fighter and attack aircraft			Strategic defense interceptors	Total combat strength[a]	Aggregate lift capacity (millions of pounds)
	Counterair	Strike	Total			
NATO						
United States	1,620	2,110	3,730	510	4,240	99
Active	1,480	1,250	2,730	130	2,860	76
Reserve	140	860	1,000	380	1,380	23
Allies	830	1,130	1,960	680	2,640	50
Total	2,450	3,240	5,690	1,190	6,880	149
Warsaw Pact						
USSR	1,200	2,800	4,000	2,900	6,900	80–90
Allies	1,500	500	2,000	...	2,000	14–16
Total	2,700	3,300	6,000	2,900	8,900	94–106

Source: William D. White, *U.S. Tactical Air Power: Missions, Forces, and Costs* (Brookings Institution, 1974), p. 115.

a. Combat aircraft only; does not include reconnaissance, electronic warfare, airlift, or support aircraft.

under the rubric of ground attack (strike) aircraft (see table A-1). These latter would include Il-28s, SU-7s, and some portion of the YAK-25, YAK-28, and MiG-17 inventories. Indeed, according to at least one source, a new SUKHOI aircraft—perhaps to be designated the SU-19— "is the first aircraft the Soviet Union has designed [specifically] for the close support mission since World War II."[3]

In sharp contrast are U.S. tactical air forces, which are geared to a much greater extent toward theater air superiority as a prerequisite to deep interdiction; however, increased emphasis on viable close support capabilities is evident in the recent decision by the U.S. Air Force to procure the A-10 close-support aircraft and the YF-16 lightweight fighter.

Thus, the assistance that Soviet tactical aviation could provide to Soviet ground forces is likely to be decidedly constrained, particularly in the area of interdiction, although because of its sheer size the Soviet tactical air force could prove a formidable competitor for air superiority on the battlefield. Moreover, the technological inferiority of the USSR vis-à-vis the West is acutely apparent in aviation, a notable example being the lack of laser- or television-guided ("smart") bombs, which promise to revolutionize the effectiveness of aerial-delivered munitions. An additional weakness that cannot be discounted is that Soviet pilots receive far less training than their U.S. or Western European counterparts, many of whom also possess the advantage of combat experience denied to all but a few Soviet pilots.

3. Steven Canby, *The Alliance and Europe, Part IV: Military Doctrine and Technology*, Adelphi Papers 109 (IISS, 1975), p. 7.